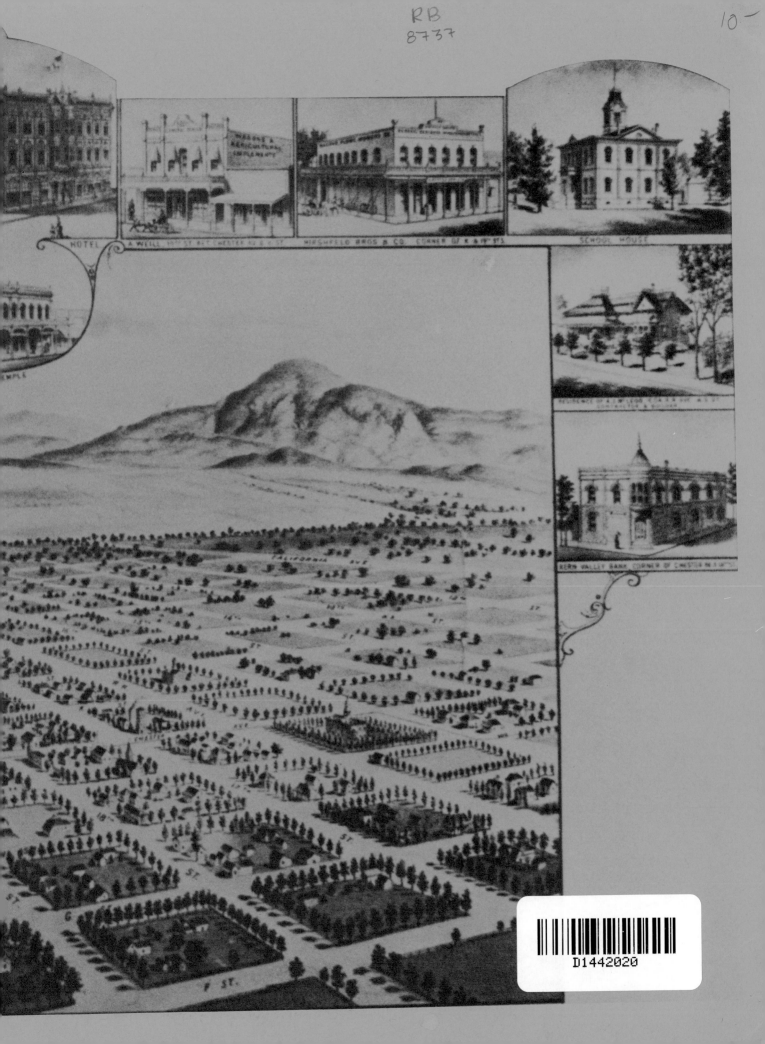

Bakersfield

WITH CONTRIBUTIONS BY
MRS. DOROTHY BAILEY,
HOWIE WINES, AND
GENE HANSON

PICTORIAL RESEARCH BY
GREGORY IGER

"PARTNERS IN PROGRESS" BY
HOWIE WINES

PRODUCED IN ASSOCIATION
WITH THE
GREATER BAKERSFIELD
CHAMBER OF COMMERCE

WINDSOR PUBLICATIONS, INC.
WOODLAND HILLS, CALIFORNIA

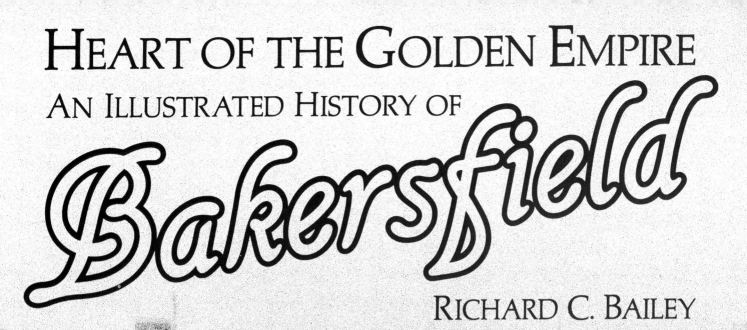

Heart of the Golden Empire
An Illustrated History of
Bakersfield

Richard C. Bailey

Windsor Publications, Inc.
History Books Division
Publisher: John M. Phillips
Design Director: Alexander D'Anca
Production Supervisor: Katherine Cooper
Senior Picture Editor: Teri Davis Greenberg
Senior Corporate History Editor: Karen Story
Marketing Director: Ellen Kettenbeil
Production Manager: Dee Cooper
Typesetting Manager: E. Beryl Myers
Proofreading Manager: Doris R. Malkin

Staff for *Heart of the Golden Empire*
Editor: Pamela Taylor
Text Editor: Taryn Bigelow
Picture Editor: Jim Mather
Corporate History Editor: Phyllis Gray
Assistant Corporate History Editor: Judith Hunter
Editorial Assistants: Patricia Buzard, Patricia Pittman, Lonnie Pham
Sales Representative: Tom Lewis
Typographers: Barbara Neiman, Cynthia Pinter
Layout Artist: Chris McKibbin
Production Artists: Connie Blaisdell, Beth Bowman

Library of Congress Cataloging in Publication Data

Bailey, Richard C., 1911-1983
    Heart of the golden empire.

    Bibliography: p.154
    Includes index.
    1. Bakersfield (Calif.) — History. 2. Bakersfield
(Calif.) — Description. 3. Bakersfield (Calif.) —
Industries. I. Title.
F869.B16B35   1984   979.4'88   84-10410
ISBN 0-89781-065-1

Acknowledgments   6

PROLOGUE

The Inland Sea and the Old People

8

CHAPTER ONE

The Trailblazers: From Fages to Frémont

12

CHAPTER TWO

The Settlers: Taming the Los Tulares

22

CHAPTER THREE

The Founders: A Thriving Town is Born

34

CHAPTER FOUR

The Warriors: Battle for the Kern

44

CHAPTER FIVE

The Rebuilders: Bakersfield Rises from Ashes

60

CHAPTER SIX

The Boomers: Riches, Roughnecks, and Rowdies

74

CHAPTER SEVEN

The Survivors: A Modern City Emerges

90

CHAPTER EIGHT

Partners in Progress

121

Patrons for *Heart of the Golden Empire*   152
Selected Bibliography   154
Index   156

ACKNOWLEDGMENTS

This book represents the conclusion of my fascination with the spirit of the West as it developed and flourished in Bakersfield and the rest of the upper San Joaquin Valley. This spirit—impatient, raw, and colorful—is still excitingly evident here.

The fascination has enveloped me for more than 50 pleasant years, filled with Old Timers' stories, crumbling treasures, and dusty volumes of memories. During that time, I've roamed the golden hills and heat-shimmering plains searching for lost trails, and known the thrill of resurrecting tattered buildings once filled with hopes and schemes. All the while I dreamed of such a book as this that would mirror in a lively, visual way the history of this remarkable area.

But in the practical sense, the book was finally made possible by the Greater Bakersfield Chamber of Commerce, an organization that has been working for Bakersfield almost since its founding. The members and executive secretary Ted Haring caught the vision of this book, sponsored it, and presented it to the community; it is their project and I am grateful. Special thanks go to those business firms who saw the enduring value of this book. Windsor Publications pulled everything together with great skill. In a work such as this the most important and difficult question is always what must be left out for want of space; my editor, Pam Taylor, has always been patient and wise in these matters.

The local team consisted mainly of Greg Iger, Howie Wines, and myself. Greg used his remarkable photographic skills to reproduce the valuable old photographs and illustrations as well as his own photographs, which add much. Howie, who knows "everyone," researched and wrote the important "Partners in Progress" chapter. Howie Wines, along with historical writer Gene Hanson, wrote the final chapter, "A Modern City Emerges." I deeply appreciate their hard work.

Always working by my side has been my faithful, darling wife, Dorothy Jean Bailey. Her indefatigable enthusiasm and talent for research and composition have more than made up for my failing strength. My daughter, Dorothy Anne Picking, served as sounding board and proofreader along with Ellen and Earl Gray. Other good friends, Evelyn Ogle and Rosalie Bollinger, labored diligently on manuscript typing. Special art work was beautifully done by Joan Henry and Patricia Embree.

Before my mind's eye marches a parade of wonderful friends who provided information for this book. I can never forget the contributions of Alphonse Weill and his family, especially Lawrence and Helen, as well as other members of the Kern County Historical Society and the reference staff of the Beale Branch, Kern County Library.

Others who should be included as important information sources are Ralph Kreiser, Dr. W. Harland Boyd, Henry Raub, Lester and Gertrude McDonald, and many more.

Contributing authors Wines and Hanson wish to acknowledge the assistance of Bakersfield's Mayor Mary K. Shell, Larry Press of the Bakersfield *Californian*, and Charlie Gravis, civic auditorium manager. In researching the oil industry stories, credit must be given to Bill Rintoul, a true historian of the oilfield rush days.

They extend additional thanks to Judge Frank Noriega, Vince Clerou, Phyllis Reischman, Margo V. Gill, researcher Molly Chanley-Covert, and Margaret Smart. Each made important contributions to that golden age of local historical recreation out of which this book grew.

RICHARD C. BAILEY
BAKERSFIELD, CALIFORNIA

Bakersfield,
Out of the lives of each
A thread is taken
And woven into your mantle.

—Rush M. Blodget,
Little Dramas of Old Bakersfield, 1931

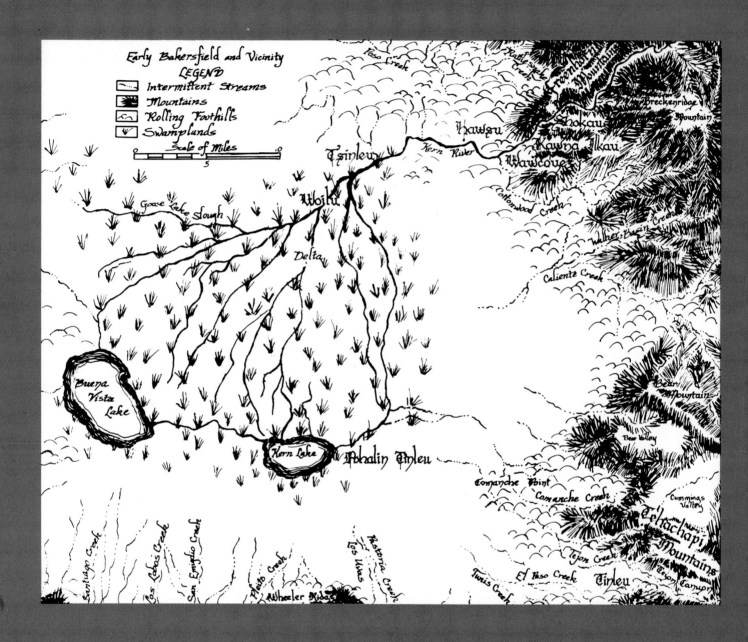

The Inland Sea

AND THE OLD PEOPLE

The people of the rancheria had a great feast over my arrival; and having regaled me well, I reciprocated to them all with tobacco and glass beads, congratulating myself on seeing the people so affable and affectionate. The young men are fine fellows, and the women very comely and clean, bathing themselves every little while; they take great care of their hair and do it up with a topknot; they wear petticoats of antelope skin and mantas of fur, though they are not very coy . . .

—Fr. Francisco Garcés, May 1, 1776

Late in the summer of 1853, William P. Blake, a geologist for the United States Topographical Corps, was searching for the most practical and economical route for a railroad across the Sierra Nevada. Since the best passes in the 450 miles of the mountains were known to be at the southern end, he and his men were carefully surveying that territory.

While studying the rounded hills just north of the Kern River, Blake picked up some fossilized shark teeth that lay exposed on the ground after a rainfall. Looking more carefully, he found other evidence that the area had once been under water.

Hundreds of millions of years ago, the region was covered by a shallow, subtropical sea. At that time the coast ranges did not yet exist and, instead of the towering Sierra Nevada, there were rolling forested hills and streams meandering down to palm-edged lagoons.

Sharks, dolphins, whales, and many other marine animals lived and died in these waters. Fossilized remains also show that elephants, giant tortoises, and other land animals were washed into this prehistoric sea from the nearby shore. (These remains would eventually break down to form vast oil and gas deposits.)

A great change came in more recent times, when volcanoes on the San Andreas Fault—the western edge of the North American plate—trembled, shook, and spewed lava. This lava formed the Coast Ranges. At the same time violent earthquakes raised the San Joaquin Valley above sea level, sloping toward the north, and the seawater drained off. The same earth movements sharply lifted the old, weathered hills on the eastern side of the valley to form the Sierra Nevada.

The climate cooled, and as the high mountains caught the clouds, snow

Early Yowlumne Indian villages in the Bakersfield vicinity have been mapped here by artist Patty Embree. Most of the sites were on the Kern River between the delta and the mountains. Courtesy, Patty Embree

accumulated on the leeward side. During the Ice Age glaciers, moving down from Mount Whitney, scoured and gouged out the old fault break that snaked across the ancient high plain and formed the deep gorge of the upper Kern River. As the climate warmed and the snow melted, new streams vigorously washed sediment into the newly formed valley. The upper San Joaquin became a series of lakes and marshes. Among them were Kern and Buena Vista lakes, but Tulare was the largest freshwater lake west of the Mississippi River.

Only 50,000 years ago, sticky tar seepages began oozing across pools of water in the low foothills on the west side of the valley. Birds and grazing animals became hopelessly mired in this tar. They, in turn, attracted carnivores in search of an easy meal. But the predators found only the same fate. These asphaltum-preserved bones show that the valley was once the home of many species that are now extinct: Columbian mammoth, saber-toothed tiger, ground sloth, several varieties of camels and horses, and the great condor-like vulture, Teratornis. But for every species that died, out there were others that flourished: tule elk, pronghorn antelope, deer, grizzly and black bear, mountain lion and wildcat, wolf and coyote, fox and weasel, otter and beaver, as well as water birds and shorebirds.

The first people appeared in this happy hunting ground only about 8,000 years ago. Refuse heaps show these early inhabitants were hunters who used the *atlatl*, a polished stone skillfully shaped so a spear could rest on it, permitting the weapon to be thrown with great force and accuracy. Later people gathered seeds for food, and became skillful at making portable milling stones for grinding.

Fairly recently, perhaps 1,000 or 2,000 years ago, newcomers speaking a different language (known as Penutian) pushed into the San Francisco Bay region and spread out from there. The largest group, the Yokuts, filled the San Joaquin Valley, or *Traw-law-win*, as they called it. This Indian nation of 50,000 was divided into tightly knit tribes—each with a name, a well-defined territory, and its own dialect.

The southeastern San Joaquin Valley was occupied by one of the largest tribes of the Yokuts nation—the Yowlumne (named for the

howl of the many white wolves in the area). Early explorers described them as a well-built, clean, and happy people, with keen senses of humor. They were excellent food gatherers, hunters of great courage, and skillful artisans.

The Yowlumne centered their existence along the dominant feature of the land—the Kern River. Villages clustered all along its course as it flowed to the valley floor. In the northeast the Yowlumne's domain extended to Sholo ("wind place"). They had no paths further up the steep, wild canyon, but downstream they speared trout from the boulders that lined the pools. The most famous site in their territory was K'ono-likin ("water's fall"), a gushing, plunging torrent as the river broke full force out of its steep canyon restrictions and into the valley. The Yowlumne, who were superstitious and lived in awe of nature, went on pilgrimages to worship at this supernatural place. This reverence for the natural world also led the Yowlumne to protect their river. They took care not to contaminate it, knowing the survival of their people down-stream depended on the purity of the drinking water. Thus the sparkling Kern roared through the valley, swift, deep, and full of fish.

Under tall sycamore trees, where Cottonwood Creek flowed into the Kern River, was the beautiful village of Wawcoye. Like most Yowlumne villages, it was laid out with military precision, in rows of small, reed-covered peaked huts with tule-mat porches in front. The huts were for sleeping only, for these were outdoor people. A fire constantly burning in front of the porch served as a center for cooking, drying hands, burning refuse, and evening singing and story-telling sessions. Cooking was done in large tight baskets by adding hot stones to the food and stirring with a looped stick. The next village, Hawsu, was on the north side of the river near the present-day location of Hart Park. Further downstream, also on the north bank almost at what became Gordon's Ferry, was the village of T'sinleu.

But the largest and most important village in the Yowlumne tribal territory was Woilu, which was situated on the present site of Bakersfield. Perched on a 15-foot knoll, it was separated by a branch of the Kern River from a smaller village on the other side. Woilu, which means "planting place" (there is evidence that

the Yowlumne practiced a primitive agriculture), was also the home of the Yowlumne's tribal chief. The village was centrally located and this enabled the chief to assure the people's safety, food supply, and civil order. Information from the lesser captains in other villages was transmitted quickly to the chief by means of smoke signals and winatun, or "messengers."

Near Woilu the Kern River divided into South Fork on the east, Old River in the middle, and into many additional channels and marshes draining into Kern and Buena Vista lakes. Throughout the delta, islands of higher land were occupied by other Yokuts villages and camps: Halaumne, Tulumne, and Tuhoumne as well as Yowlumne. The villagers were all friendly and intermarriage was common.

The Yokuts were well adapted to making the most of their land. Tules and other marsh plants grew so abundantly in and around the river, lakes, and swamps, that the whole southern San Joaquin was known as the "valley of tules." The plants grew to at least ten feet and gave the Yowlumne food, fiber, and, most interestingly, a means of transportation. Craftsmen made beautiful tule canoes with upturned prows by lashing together fat bundles of tules. These light skiffs held heavy supplies and would accommodate several people.

The lakes and swamps of the delta provided abundant food. A choice wild rice was harvested as well as cattails and other valuable swamp plants. Otters, beavers, raccoons, and turtles were plentiful and delicious. Yowlumne fishing groups lived all summer on the lakes, using tule rafts equipped with a hole through which to spear fish; nets brought up more.

Further east along the edges of the valley and in the foothills, where the land was higher and drier, thousands of tule elk, deer, and pronghorn antelope grazed or wheeled wildly over the plains. The Yowlumne skillfully hunted these and other animals with a few well-placed arrows. The bear was considered a brother, however, spoken of respectfully and seldom hunted. They also held large rabbit drives and made cloaks, skirts, and warm blankets out of the fur.

Trade had flourished among the Yokuts not only because of a unified system of exchange (shell and steatite bead money with established values) but also because a single language was common to the entire valley. The Yowlumne and other southern tribes had an advantage in this commerce since the best routes out of the valley were through their region. They traded their fine woven baskets, animal pelts, asphaltum, and other Yokuts products for shells from the Pacific Coast. They also ranged through the Mojave Desert for obsidian, a volcanic glass very valuable in the valley for making arrow points and knives. Eventually, the trade trails became deeply worn from centuries of Indian use. But these same trails, the symbols of Yowlumne prosperity, would soon bring the first of white men—Spaniards and later Americans would alter the Indians' placid existence forever.

The Trailblazers

FROM FAGES TO FRÉMONT

The area that now comprises Kern County has an interesting history dating back to a time before the Declaration of Independence. Containing as it does the only all-year passes through the Sierra Nevada, it was the crossroads of the Spaniard, the Mexican, and the American coming from or going to the interior.

—Spanish Trailblazers in the South San Joaquin
Jesse D. Stockton, Glendon J. Rodgers, W. Harland Boyd, 1957

John C. Frémont made a career in the U.S. Army and used most of that career in thorough explorations of the American West. He had much influence on the United States' decision to annex California. Courtesy, Cirker, Dictionary of American Portraits, *Dover, 1969*

In 1772 the Spanish had only a three-year-old outpost at San Diego. The San Joaquin Valley was a vast unknown to them. Two deserters from the Spanish military forces were the first "new people" to enter the valley. Commander Pedro Fages and his band of "leatherjackets" followed in pursuit. They didn't find the runaways, but they did find a beautiful new land. The first Indian village they saw, Fages called Buena Vista Rancheria.

Spain had claimed all of this territory some 250 years earlier when Hernando Cortez captured and plundered Mexico. But, aside from several aborted attempts to establish a port in Alta California, the Spaniards showed little interest in the area until 1765. That year King Charles III of Spain found out Russian fur traders were hunting seal on the Alta California coast, and decided it was time to establish colonies in the northern territory before some other country did.

When the governor of Mexico, José de Gálvez, received the king's order "to guard the dominions from all invasion and insult," he revived dreams of exploring and settling San Diego and Monterey. But de Gálvez did more than dream. He planned a chain of Franciscan missions in Alta California and put Don Gaspar de Portolá and Fr. Junípero Serra in charge of launching the endeavor.

At the beginning of the Spanish occupation, there were several hundred thousand Indians, and never more than 300 armed and mounted Spanish soldiers to subdue them. The soldiers were unwittingly aided in their cause by contagious diseases they introduced to the natives, diseases for which the natives had no immunity.

Under these circumstances, the Spanish at first had great difficulty attracting colonists to their little settlements. Only self-sacrificing priests came willingly to Alta California in those days. There were no opportunities for quick wealth. There was only danger and isolation as the outposts were cut off from essential protection and supplies. If colonists

Padre Francisco Garcés (left) came to the Bakersfield area in 1776. This painting depicts the massacre of both Padre Garcés and Padre Barreneche on July 19, 1781, on the California side of the Colorado River. Courtesy, Clarence Cullimore

were to be induced to settle in Alta California, reliable supply routes were a necessity. Capt. Juan Bautista de Anza took matters into his own hands. Since the closest source of supply was the Mexican state of Sonora, he planned a trail from there to Monterey, by now the Mexican capital of Alta California. Fr. Francisco Garcés, who had already explored much of the way, was assigned to go along.

Father Garcés' own mission territory was southern Arizona, but he was indefatigably peripatetic, exploring and ministering to all the Indians he could possibly reach during his short life. Although fear of the Indians spurred most Spaniards to travel with military escorts, Garcés traveled alone, armed only with a few gifts, a compass, and a Christian banner.

Padre Pedro Font, a strict and humorless chaplain who knew Father Garcés well, wrote:

Father Garcés is so well fitted to get along with the Indians and go among them that he appears to be an Indian himself. Like the Indians he is phlegmatic in everything. He sits with them in the circle, or at night along the fire, with his legs crossed. . . . And although the foods of the Indians are as nasty and dirty as those outlandish people themselves, the Father eats with great gusto, and says they are good for the stomach, and very fine. In short, God has created him, as I see it, solely for the purpose of

seeking out those unhappy and rustic people.

Early expeditions had gone through the forbidding desert between Yuma and San Gabriel, then followed El Camino Real to get to Monterey. Thinking there had to be a better route, Spanish authorities encouraged Father Garcés to explore the Indian trails up the Colorado River for a more direct route to Monterey.

On a fine spring day in April 1776, Garcés strode into the San Joaquin Valley accompanied only by his faithful donkey and an old Yokuts Indian who had once lived there. They headed north through what is today the Arvin area. As Garcés went along he made friends as usual with all the Indians he encountered, despite warnings that he probably would not get out of the valley alive. When the energetic Father reached the Kern River, he set down the first written description of its waters:

May 1: Having gone one league northwest I came upon a large river which made much noise, at the outlet of the Sierra de San Marcos [Sierra Nevada], and whose waters, crystalline, bountiful, and palatable, flowed on a course from the east through a straightened channel [Kern River].

Some of the ''hostile'' natives assisted him in crossing:

They asked me if I knew how to swim, and I answered them nay; I supplicated them they should make me a raft, and they answered that they knew not. At last they ordered me to undress, which I did, down to shirt and drawers; they insisted that I should put off every garment, but this I refused to do. They conveyed me across between four of them swimming, two taking me by the arms and the other two by the body; whereupon I took advantage of the occasion to bathe at my pleasure in that water so limpid and beautiful. . . . This famous river . . . I named Rio de San Felipe [Kern River].

Heading north, Garcés crossed Poso Creek, treading through flower-strewn foothills to the present locale of Woody. He reached the White River, east of Delano, where he performed the first Christian baptism in the valley. He found another Indian, a runaway from one of the coastal missions who told him in Spanish of shootings and floggings there.

Garcés then turned southeast, hoping to find the source of Kern River. He got as far as Kern Canyon but, running out of time, had to turn around. (The padre's Indian guides would not enter the San Joaquin Valley with him, and he had told them he would return in four or five days.) The water was too high to recross by any means so he continued downstream on the north side of the Kern River. He passed north of what is now the Garcés traffic circle on Bakersfield's Chester Avenue. As he pressed on, Garcés noted "the extent of woodland, pasturage, and fitness for irrigation," and he proceeded to pen the first written words about the future site of Bakersfield.

I arrived at a rancheria [a portion of Woilu] which could contain 150 souls, in which place runs the river now divided in two branches and has the bed wider, so wide that they have been able to make a bridge of two trunks of alders, which serve for the crossing, though at some hazard. The branch of this river, which passes immediately by the rancheria, takes a course to the west-northwest, and they told me that lower down it turns to the north till it unites with that very large river [San Joaquin River]. The other branch of this river, which is smaller, flows to the west, discharging its waters where they are swollen over some very fertile plains, in which are formed large lagunas and marshes. The place, which has beautiful hills for the situation of missions free from all inundation, I named San Miguel de los Noches por Santo Principe, one of the patrons of the expedition.

Garcés left the San Joaquin Valley on May 11, 1776 by way of Cumming's Valley, Tehachapi Valley, and the Oak Creek Pass. He did not have the opportunity to search further for the headwaters of the Rio de San Felipe (Kern River) as he had wished. But he saw enough to visualize the San Joaquin as a great agricultural area and the Rio de San Felipe as the key to transportation between the Pacific Ocean and the Southwest.

In August 1779 Garcés was ordered back to the Yuma area, for there was trouble with the Indians. Fed up with their mistreatment at the hands of the Spanish, on July 17, 1781, the Yumas rioted, killing Spanish soldiers and many settlers. The Indians' chief, Palma,

Local artist Patty Embree composed this drawing of a Kern County Indian with an atlatl (spearthrower) stalking a tule elk. Courtesy, Patty Embree

interceded for his beloved Father Garcés. Nevertheless, two days later, Garcés and three other priests were clubbed to death by the Indians. Garcés was 43.

Tension between the Spanish and the Indians had been building ever since the Spaniards had arrived. From the native viewpoint, about the only benefit of the Spanish presence was the introduction of the horse. The first horses had been brought in by fugitive Spanish soldiers, who also brought cattle and firearms. The horses and longhorns thrived on the nutritious grasses of the foothills and soon formed great wild herds in the valley. The Indians had a keen appreciation for this Spanish gift. They became expert horsemen and even developed a taste for roasted horse flesh.

The Indians also used their new-found mobility to strike back at the Spaniards. From the Tulares and over the Coast Ranges they would swoop down on the missions and ranches, returning with more horses and anything else of value. In response the missions and ranches badgered New Spain's government to establish missions and a presidio (fort) in the valley. Repeated scouting trips were made to pick out sites for the grand project and as a result, a great deal of the valley was explored.

The most notable of these expeditions came in 1806. Lieutenant Gabriel Moraga and 25 soldiers went from Mission San Juan Baptista down the less explored eastern side of the valley. The party discovered and named the Merced, Tuolumne, Stanislaus, Calaveras, and Mokelumne rivers. Eventually they reached the Rio de San Felipe (Kern River). They left the valley by the Tejon Pass on their way to Mission San Fernando. (On one of Moraga's many later trips, he discovered and named the San Joaquin River for the father of the Virgin Mary. Since this name was eventually applied to the whole valley, the honor of naming the San Joaquin Valley belongs in a sense to Moraga.)

But development of Alta California was put on hold again when the French monarchy fell to Napoleon and 100,000 Frenchmen invaded Spain. In 1808 Joseph Bonaparte, Napoleon's brother, was placed on the Spanish throne. The government of New Spain pledged its support

to the exiled Ferdinand VII. Now the existing missions there received no funds for even token protection. Indeed, the missions were expected to contribute to the Spanish war effort.

England took armed offense at Napoleon's imperialism and the conflict soon spread to include the United States as well. The War of 1812 finally was resolved in 1814 at the Treaty of Ghent and Ferdinand VII was restored to the Spanish throne. But the war had left the Spaniards weakened and colonial leaders in New Spain could expect little support from the mother country.

Although informed of the situation in Spain and Mexico, Spanish fathers continued to request missions in the San Joaquin while the rancheros on the coast still hoped for a presidio to protect them from Indian raids.

An independence movement swept through the Spanish colonies after 1810, spurred by the weakness of the Spanish monarchy. The dispatch announcing Mexico's independence from Spain reached the California capital of Monterey early in 1822. The council in Monterey swore allegiance to the new Mexican government. But this did not change the problems in Alta California. It had been almost 50 years since Father Garcés' original vision of the southern valley as a key to interior prosperity. The hope was still alive, but now Mexico had even less of a capacity for realizing that dream than Spain had shown earlier.

The determining influence in the battle for control of Alta California, however, was just over the horizon. In November 1826 an unusual young man, an American, made his way down the Colorado River and found an Indian village well-known to Garcés. The Indians welcomed the man and his small group of trappers (the first Americans they had seen), helped them across the Colorado River, and sent them on their way with guides who would lead them through California's Mojave Desert. The leader of this party was Jedediah Strong Smith, a remarkable young man, as unusual on the American frontier as Garcés had been on the Spanish frontier. Two years before, he had been the first American to demonstrate the value of the South Pass over the Continental Divide, proving it was the easiest and safest trail over the Rocky Mountains.

Crossing the impregnable, parched Mojave

Another drawing by Patty Embree shows a cluster of Yowlumne huts on the bank of the Kern River. Courtesy, Patty Embree

Desert was difficult. Desperately in need of supplies, Smith's party rode down from the encircling mountains to the San Bernardino Valley. Half-starved and ragged, they resembled scarecrows on exhausted horses. To say that their appearance out of the Mojave was a surprise is to put it mildly. This dashed Mexico's confidence that the deserts would keep invaders from approaching Alta California land. To prove that he had really taken this route, Smith lent his journey diary to Governor José M. Echeandía of Alta California; it has not been recovered to this day. The padres of the San Gabriel Mission were kind and cordial to Smith and his men, but the governor suspected the Americans of being soldiers and spies for the United States government. Had he known that Jedediah Smith's reports would fling wide the door to the Pacific Coast to the hated Americans, the governor would have let them all rot in prison.

He was very reluctant to grant the necessary passport for travel to Smith and his men. Instead, after much indecision, Governor Echeandía only ordered them to leave California by the same route by which they had entered.

They left on February 1, 1827. Smith felt he had complied by leaving San Gabriel Mission the same way he had come, retracing their way across the Cajon Pass. From there, however, he turned west, searching for water. He entered the southern San Joaquin Valley on February 5, 1827. The first American visitor there, he wrote in his journal:

I arrived at a Lake called by the Spaniards Too Larree or Flag Lake [Kern Lake]. . . . Too Larree Lake is about 12 miles in circumference and is in a fine large valley which commences about 12 miles South of it . . . The following day in moving along the bank of the Lake I surprised some Indians who

The legendary mountain man Jed Smith was one of the first Americans to explore the Kern County area. Courtesy, Cirker, Dictionary of American Portraits, *Dover, 1969*

immediately pushed out into the lake in canoes or rather rafts made of flag. My guide succeeded in getting them to return to the shore. One of them could talk some Spanish and I engaged him for a guide. I watered my horses and got some fish from the Indians (who I observed had some horses stolen no doubt from the Spaniards). . . . These Indians call themselves Wa-ya-la-ma.

Smith had found the Yowlumne Yokuts Indians. He was probably near Woilu, the future site of Bakersfield, where he was cordially received and was able to replenish his supplies.

Smith next turned his attention to the financial portion of his expedition. Skirting the foothills, trapping beaver in the streams that flowed out of the Sierra Nevada and shooting an occasional elk or antelope for food, Smith moved his men as rapidly as possible. It was spring, and he hurried to rendezvous with his business partners in the Rockies.

By April, having secured several packs of beaver, he pressed up the Stanislaus River hoping to find a pass through the Sierra. Finding only hostile Indians and deep snow, Smith was forced to turn back. He left his men at Knight's Ferry, but on May 20 Smith set out again with two companions in a second attempt to surmount the Sierra. They followed the approximate course of the present Route 4, with, remarkably, neither map nor guide. The three men then began the trek across what would become Nevada toward the Great Salt Lake, the first white men to cross Nevada.

After meeting his partners in the Rocky Mountains, Smith quickly gathered up provisions and 17 men for his return to California. He retraced his steps, crossing the Colorado at an Indian village he had passed through before. But this time the Indians killed ten of Smith's men and stole all the group's furs and equipment. Nevertheless, Smith picked out the trail across the Mojave Desert from memory, traveling rapidly for fear of the Indians. Restocking at a ranch in the San Bernardino Valley, the remaining men hurried through Yokuts country. Smith reached his former party at Knight's Ferry on September 18, 1829.

This time when he reached Monterey, however, the Mexican government detained Smith for several months, accusing him of claiming country in the San Joaquin Valley. It was not until November 15 that he finally wriggled free of this situation and, reprovisioning again, eventually headed north for Hudson's Bay Company territory. Finally, well out of Alta California, Smith and his men were harrassed by many Indians along the Pacific Coast. On July 14, 1828, the Kelawatset Indians murdered the whole party, except for Smith and two other men. They wandered for almost a month, until they found Fort Vancouver on the Columbia River, the great post of the Hudson's Bay Company. The English company, remarkably, retrieved all the furs and other property stolen from Smith's party by the Indians. The British purchased them from Smith and aided him in refitting for his return to the Rockies.

The price for this assistance was an examination of Smith's expedition journals and the freedom to copy his maps. The Hudson's Bay Company took immediate advantage of this information and extended its trapping into California, even to the Kern River and further south. Smith, too, made use of the encounter, reporting his sharp observations of the British post to the American government.

By 1830 Smith and his partners had done well enough to sell out their fur company and retire. Smith bought a house in St. Louis and continued to work on his maps and journals. On a trading expedition to Santa Fe the next year, Smith was killed by a Comanche Indian. He was only 30 years old, but he had done more than any other mountain man to open up the West and acquaint the world with the southern San Joaquin Valley. He had proven that the southern route was the only expedient way around the rugged and dangerous Sierra Nevada. And, just as Mexican authorities had feared, Smith's maps and accounts were widely published and encouraged other Americans to follow.

In 1830 another trapper named Ewing Young entered the southern San Joaquin, following the same desert trail that Fr. Francisco Garcés and Jedediah Smith had traveled, and trapped around the Kern River. In his party was 20-year-old Kit Carson, who would return many times to Kern County.

But the era of great fortunes from beaver was short-lived. The main use of the little skins had been for gentlemen's beaver hats, and they became almost obsolete as the silk top hat became fashionable. It was perhaps just as well, for the rodent was rapidly becoming extinct in North America.

One who tried his luck at beaver a bit late was Captain Bonneville during a leave of absence from the army. During the summer of 1833, he sent Joseph Reddeford Walker, one of the most famous mountain men, to reconnoiter the country west of the Great Salt Lake. Walker took his party to the Pacific Coast and returned by way of the southern San Joaquin Valley. In the spring of 1834, he and his men passed through the present site of Bakersfield, turned up the Kern River, and climbed the Greenhorn Mountains. Walker and his men were the first white men to travel through the fine pass in this part of the Sierras, the northernmost all-weather pass through the great mountain range. It soon became known as Walker's Pass and later was an important gateway for gold-seekers and settlers.

Washington Irving, using Bonneville's journals and maps, wrote *The Adventures of Captain Bonneville, U.S.A., in the Rocky*

Kit Carson was another of the early explorers who helped open the West to pioneers. Courtesy, Cirker, Dictionary of American Portraits, *Dover, 1969*

Mountains and the Far West. It was a vivid adventure story with the most accurate maps of the times and was an immediate best-seller.

Nonetheless the wonders of the Golden West mesmerized adventurous Americans. Although California was still in Mexican hands, parties of American settlers set out on the dangerous journey across the Rocky Mountains, the desert, and the Sierra Nevada. Most of those fortunate enough to survive the journey did so with the help of experienced guides—mountain men of the fur-trapping days.

The first group of Yankee settlers to come through the southern San Joaquin Valley was organized by Joseph B. Chiles, who had come to California with the first emigrants in 1841. Chiles' party left Independence, Missouri, in May 1843. The group consisted of 30 men and a few women and children. This was the first wagon train of emigrants to cross the Rocky Mountains. Veteran mountain man Joseph Reddeford Walker was their guide. He led them down the route he had discovered in 1834, taking the wagon train east of the Sierra past Mono Lake. Within a week Walker had guided the party over Walker's Pass and down into the

Using the materials they found in the area, Yokuts Indians made tule canoes for travel on the local waterways. Courtesy, Patty Embree

San Joaquin Valley. These emigrants, however, traveled north to what later became known as Gilroy.

While seasoned mountain men such as Walker could help handsful of settlers through, the American government knew that accurate maps were necessary to encourage large-scale emigration. To accomplish this task, the Americans selected John Charles Frémont, a brilliant young adventurer. As a lieutenant in the United States Topographical Corps, he had proven his capability in reports on South Pass and the trail through the Rockies.

The purpose of Frémont's second western expedition, which began in 1843, was the mapping of the Oregon Trail and the land south of the Columbia River. Despite the February cold and snow, they mapped the Oregon Trail, then dropped down to get a profile of the Sierra Nevada around Lake Tahoe, finally reaching Sutter's Fort.

The party then proceeded down the San Joaquin Valley, reaching the Kern River on April 12, 1844, at which time Frémont commented, "It is about thirty-five yards wide, with a stony and gravelly bed, and the swiftest stream we have crossed since leaving the bay."

They continued easterly near the foothills, and, searching for Walker's Pass, they turned into Tehachapi Pass. They ascended Caliente Creek and selected a campsite. To their surprise a Spanish-speaking Indian rode into their camp. The next day he joined the group and showed Frémont the way over Oak Creek Pass and onto the Old Spanish Trail toward the Colorado River.

When Frémont returned to Washington, he quickly prepared his report, which he presented to the War Department on March 1, 1845. Congress and the whole country were delighted with the new maps and the wealth of practical advice for the emigrant. It was quickly published and was a great stimulus to the westward movement both in the U.S. and abroad.

By this time Americans had been seized by the desire to possess the entire continent. War was expected with Mexico over the annexation of Texas. And it was resolved that England's flimsy presence in the Northwest not be allowed to spread into Oregon or California. Before even completing his second expedition report, Frémont received orders for a third western assignment. He selected 60 dedicated, loyal sharpshooters, including Joseph Reddeford Walker, Alexis Godey, and Kit Carson. But one young man in the party was quite different. This was Edward Meyer Kern, a Philadelphian. He was in no sense a mountain man—he had hardly traveled. He was only 23, but he was a talented artist who could produce accurate pictures. Even though he had no training in topography, he was selected over 40 other applicants because of the accuracy of the drawings he submitted to Frémont and because of friends who spoke highly of him. Kern quickly learned from Frémont the use of instruments and the techniques of topography and mapping. Popular among the men, Kern, known as Ned, was tall and thin with dark red, curly hair. His gray eyes were said to be sad, but no matter how hard the going he always had a ready wit. Frémont eventually honored this young man by naming the Kern River after him.

The expedition pushed off from the Midwest on June 23, 1845. It turned out to be the most thorough investigation yet of the Great Basin. All current maps described the area as a "sandy and barren wasteland," but these explorers found instead a series of ranges, each with grazing land, game, and water.

When the group reached Walker Lake at the base of the passes over the Sierra, the party divided. Frémont took a few men, hoping to map a new pass, and headed up the Truckee River. He found the South Fork of the American River, and reached the San Joaquin Valley in a week. Walker led the main party south along the Sierra escarpment, then turned west up the easy ascent of Walker Pass. Kern wrote in his journal of snow in Hot Springs Valley and not much to eat. It wasn't a cheerful New Year's. Nevertheless, they happily looked from the snowy Greenhorn Mountains to the sunny valley below. Waiting for Frémont, the group later camped on the Kern River, where the hunting was good.

On January 18, 1846, with no sign of their leader, the men broke camp and moved north. They finally found Frémont at San Jose. Frémont and his riflemen in the ensuing months backed American settlers in their rebellion against Mexico. In July a group of Americans chose Frémont to direct the new "Republic of California," until United States

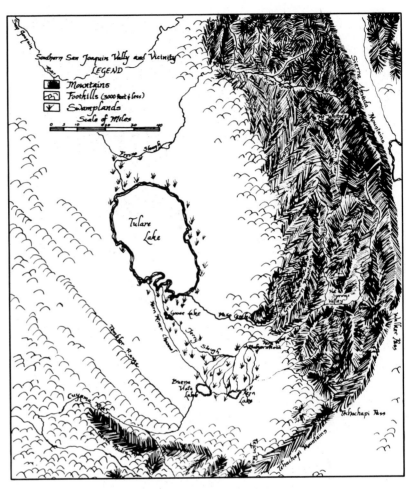

This Patty Embree map details the Southern Sierra and Kern River watershed. Courtesy, Patty Embree

troops, in a series of disorganized clashes with the Mexicans, brought California into the American fold. With the defeat of Mexico, the 1848 Treaty of Guadalupe Hidalgo gave the United States a huge tract of land that included modern-day Texas, Arizona, Nevada, California, Utah, and parts of New Mexico, Colorado, and Wyoming.

But before the treaty was formally signed on January 24, 1848, a discovery was made at Sutter's Mill on the American River. Lt. Edward F. Beale arrived in Washington with reports of the discovery of gold, and he brought specimens. Newspapers spread the word. But the best publicity came from President James Polk, who reported the find in his annual message to Congress. Soon 230 ounces of California gold were on public display at the War Department. It is estimated that by 1851, 100,000 people had rushed to the goldfields. The land of the Yowlumne would never be the same.

The Settlers

TAMING THE LOS TULARES

I traveled west to Tejon Pass along the foothills, and was as you can imagine highly impressed with the country. There was considerable grass and wild game, but not a single human being did we see. I bought this forty thousand acre tract and started to raise cattle. In those days my nearest neighbors were at Visalia on one side and at Los Angeles on the other.

—Gen. Edward Fitzgerald Beale, 1857,
from Decatur House, *by Marie Beale, 1954*

Carlton Watkins made two trips to the Bakersfield area at the end of the 19th century. One of the photographs from his trips is this landscape of the Kern River near the mouth of the canyon showing the formidable country the pioneers faced. Courtesy, Beale Memorial Library

Most of the overland gold-seekers rushed to California by the most established route, the California Trail. But a few prospectors, wishing to avoid the High Sierra, took the Old Spanish Trail. This southerly route was by far the best way, according to Los Angeles storekeepers (who wanted the business). They felt that better roads between Los Angeles and the San Joaquin would mean more travelers would take that route to the northern California goldfields.

So in 1850 a party of gold-seekers from Los Angeles was engaged to work on the road from the San Fernando Valley, by way of San Francisquito Canyon, Elizabeth Lake, and Tejon Canyon, and then continuing down the eastern side of the San Joaquin Valley. It became known as the Los Angeles-Stockton road. That same year, George H. Derby of the United States Topographical Corps, was scouting for a military post site. He traveled south along a portion of the Los Angeles and Stockton route and predicted it would become very popular.

But Derby's enthusiasm did not extend to the valley. Even after the discovery of gold in 1848 and statehood in 1850, there was no rush to the San Joaquin. Most early surveys, including Derby's, reported no sign of life. Derby saw only mosquitoes, swamps, dust storms, and vast emptiness, describing it as a "most miserable country."

But these early reports were not correct. Although many of the numerous Indian villages reported by Fages 100 years before were gone, the Indian population, though greatly reduced, had not vanished. Although Indians were as incidental to most Americans as sagebrush and easily overlooked, these early travelers also missed several non-Indian communities.

For example, the village of San Emigdio had a written record that went back to 1824. It was a stopping point on El Camino Viejo, the first wagon road from the Pueblo de Los Angeles to

San Francisco. The village was situated where San Emigdio Canyon gradually slopes into the plains, with a population of Spanish, Mexican, American, French, and Russian settlers, as well as Indians. It was a collection of adobe homes surrounded by gardens. There was a church, a cemetery, and a few stores.

Perhaps the group of Mexican families south of the Indian village of Woilu couldn't be called a village. But some of these people had emigrated as early as 1846 and worked hard to build homes and ranches. Ventura Cuen brought his family from Sonora in 1849 and built his home just north of the others. As often as possible a traveling padre stopped to teach the children, the first known schooling in the area. In Gold Rush days the settlement became known as Panama because it was thought malaria had been introduced there by someone who had been infected in the Isthmus of Panama.

The early surveys also failed to show that there were approximately 203,898 acres in the southern San Joaquin Valley and Tehachapi Mountain area of choice land unavailable to Americans because the Mexican government had already given them as land grants to the specially favored. The Treaty of Guadalupe Hidalgo was specific about the obligation to protect existing Mexican property rights. After involved legal consideration, all five land grants were declared valid: Rancho San Emigdio, Rancho Castaic, Rancho El Tejon, Rancho La Liebre, and Rancho Los Alamos y Agua Caliente. These grants did not cause as much dissatisfaction as did those in other parts of California. Few people stayed in the San Joaquin, preferring to pass through as quickly as possible.

This was due in part to the Indians who inhabited the region from the White River to Kern Lake, who were making concerted attacks on miners, settlers, and travelers. In 1851 a whole trail herd of 2,000 cattle was run off and several vaqueros were killed. This was considered especially serious by southern Californians. Their main income came from driving their herds north through the southern San Joaquin and selling them in San Francisco and further north at the mines. In response Congress set up an Indian Commission, but the legislators refused to approve any of the agreements reached.

In 1852 enough settlers around Three Rivers had survived the Indian depredations to justify the creation of Tulare County from the southern half of huge Mariposa County and the northern part of Los Angeles County. The

The San Emigdio Ranch was one of the original Mexican land grants in the San Joaquin Valley. Its ownership went uncontested after the Treaty of Guadalupe Hidalgo because of the perceived undesirability of the area. Courtesy, Beale Memorial Library; Carlton Watkins Photo

A farm couple in Tejon Ranch posed for this Carlton Watkins photo in 1889. Courtesy, Beale Memorial Library

first county seat was in Woodsville, in a log cabin on the south side of the Kaweah River. Just the year before Indians had skinned John Woods alive in that cabin and had killed the rest of the nearby settlers. Col. Thomas Baker, who would be so important to Bakersfield, was then busy surveying the new little town of Visalia, which soon took over as the Tulare County seat. Major Aneas B. Gordon was named the county recorder. He decided to open a ferry over the Kern River where the Los Angeles-Stockton road crossed. Gordon was granted a franchise to operate the ferry below the China Grade bluff, where he pulled a flatboat by cable between two small adobe buildings. The ferry was a great help to travelers, who previously would have had to stop, contrive a boat for their possessions and cargo, and then attempt to swim their horses across. All this had to be done in clear view of thieves and murderers, as well as rampaging Indians.

Outlaws were such a problem that the California legislature organized a group of Rangers and offered a reward of $3,000 for the capture of one of the most dangerous marauders, Joaquin Murieta. Harry Love was named leader of the 20 or 25 Rangers. There are many accounts of Joaquin Murieta's capture. One version claims the Rangers tracked Murieta almost to Kern Lake, where they spied a puff of smoke behind a draw. There they found 15 men about to prepare a meal. The band was armed only with knives, but they looked enough like the outlaws to the Rangers. So they killed the two men they thought were Joaquin Murieta and his supposed accomplice, Three Fingered Jack. The head of Murieta and the hand of Three Fingered Jack were preserved in a keg of brandy. There was some doubt that the head in the jar belonged to Murieta, but the Rangers were rewarded $1,000 to divide, plus expenses. Their captain, Harry Love, received an extra $5,000 from a grateful legislature.

The problem of Murieta was out of the way, but the problem of the Indians was not. The congressional rejection of proposed treaties hadn't helped anyone. The Indians faced starvation and extinction, and posed a grave danger to settlers. Into this tragic situation came Edward Fitzgerald Beale, who was appointed by President Millard Fillmore as Superintendent of Indian Affairs in California and Nevada. Ned Beale, a native of Bloomingdale in the District of Columbia, was a young man from a wealthy, influential family with proper connections. But he was also a genuine Westerner. He knew the problems of the settlers and those attempting to build a new

Gordon's Ferry was an overhead cable ferry operated during the 1850s by Major Gordon. An adobe station house was located on the south bank of the Kern River, just a few yards to the west of this bridge. The house also served as a station on the Butterfield Overland Mail Stage route from 1858 to 1860. Photo by Gregory Iger

state. And he had compassion for the Indians.

Beale adopted a plan for the Indians that incorporated the best of the mission system and the best of the reservation system. First, a garrison of soldiers would protect both the Indians and the settlers, thus maintaining peace on the California-Nevada frontier. In March 1853 Congress set aside $250,000 for five military reservations. Second, Beale moved to set up a pilot Indian reservation. He enlisted the help of Lt. Robert Williamson of the United States Topographical Corps. Williamson, who was surveying the passes out of the southern San Joaquin Valley for a railroad route, and Beale, jointly selected Tejon Canyon as the ideal place for the experimental reservation. The site they chose had been the location of the Yowlumne Yokuts village of Tinleu. The area had a stable Indian population that practiced agriculture introduced by refugees from missions. An adjacent canyon had a beautiful site for a military fort, well situated to protect the Los Angeles-Stockton road. Both sites were approved as Sebastian Indian Reservation and Fort Tejon.

The reservation was a great success under Beale. The Indians liked and trusted him. Sam Bishop, for whom the city of Bishop was later named, was in charge of the reservation's farming operation. The *Daily Alta California* reported in 1854 that the Indian raids had stopped. It stated that 2,500 Indians on the reservation had harvested 42,000 bushels of wheat and 10,000 bushels of barley. These amounts they turned over to the federal government, keeping enough additional grain to satisfy their own needs.

The reservation was so successful under Beale that local settlers complained. They said too much land was set aside for the Indians, creating unfair competition for their farms. Beale also aroused ill feelings because he would not tolerate a dishonest Indian agent and dismissed several, who became vindictive enemies. This bitterness resulted in a plan to get rid of Beale. The federal government charged Beale with misuse of government funds and he was suddenly removed from office. But Beale had kept meticulous records. The subsequent trial resulted in the disgrace of his accusers and the complete clearing of his name. A series of superintendents followed, none of whom were

very successful or appreciated. It was an impossible and thankless job.

Before Beale was discharged, he also was instrumental in the establishment of Fort Tejon about 15 miles southwest of the Indian reservation, near the present-day community of Lebec. An important southern California freighter and stagecoach operator, Phineas Banning, and his partner, David W. Alexander, a Los Angeles businessman, were awarded the freighting contract and brought in supplies for the fort's construction and maintenance. Fort Tejon developed into the chief military, social, and political center between Millerton and Los Angeles. At the height of its activity in the late 1850s there were more than 20 buildings at the post, and the dragoons saw action all over the western United States. Both reservation and the fort received scant attention during the Civil War, and were completely abandoned in 1864.

But at their peak, the Sebastian Indian Reservation and the dragoons at the fort changed the region into an area where travel and settlement were possible. And it had happened just in time, for gold fever had reached the Greenhorn Mountains, east of the

Kern Delta. As early as 1851 gold had been discovered on the White River and attracted several hundred prospectors. Some of the miners sought the gold by burrowing into the riverbanks and surrounding hills. These diggings were called "wolf holes" and a few still exist.

But the real rush to the Kern River came in 1855 after Richard Keyes, a leading miner, discovered the Keyes Mine near Hogeye, soon renamed Keyesville. It quickly became a small town with shanty stores in the center, and miners' cabins haphazardly straggling up the slopes. In Los Angeles the March 1855 issue of *The Southern Californian* announced:

Stop the Press! Glorious News from Kern River! Bring Out the Big Guns! There are a thousand gulches rich with gold and room for ten thousand miners. Miners average $50 a day. Five men in ten days took out $4,500.

Men dropped everything as they had in 1849. In four months 6,000 fortune-seekers arrived in the upper Kern River Valley. This gave rise to the mountain communities of Glennville, Quartzburg, Bodfish, Havilah, and others.

The population influx inspired Col. Thomas Baker, then a member of the California Assembly from Tulare County, to propose a new county. He introduced a bill to create "Buena Vista County" out of the southern part of Tulare County. The bill passed but the gold miners couldn't spare the time for the necessary business to make it law. So Buena Vista County languished. Nevertheless, it appeared on maps for several years.

Phineas Banning, meanwhile, with his usual quick response to opportunity, extended his freight line up to Kern River Falls, where the river left its canyon and flowed into the valley. Food, equipment, whiskey, and other essentials had to be packed the rest of the way by mule, a very expensive operation.

Some of the less successful miners decided they could make a more certain income hunting and selling meat to those busy prospecting. An opportunity for those with a lot of nerve lay in killing the grizzly bears that were a hazard to the miners. James Capen Adams (popularized as "Grizzly Adams" in

Ned Beale first came to California as the area's Superintendent of Indian Affairs. He tried to humanely balance the needs of the settlers and Indians. Courtesy, Kern County Museum

The Lebec Tree, under
which Peter Lebec was
buried, was carved with the
epitaph of the early
pioneer. The piece of bark
was removed to an exhibit
at the Fort Tejon museum.
Courtesy, Ticor

The guardhouse (left) and
another building are part of
the adobe ruins at Fort
Tejon, now a historical
park. Courtesy, Beale
Memorial Library

film and television) hunted in the Greenhorn
Mountains at this time. Some of these early
suppliers were the first to settle in the Kern
River area. One Greenhorn Indian-trader-
turned-hunter was Thomas Fitzgerald, who it
was said, came with Joseph Reddeford Walker
in 1834. He had also been one of Frémont's
riflemen. Fitzgerald had built an adobe Indian
trading post in Glennville, the oldest existing
trading post in Kern County. He also had a
small lodge on Kern Island, which he used
when hunting for tule elk.

Ranchers elsewhere heard about the need for
meat, as well as the fine grazing in the southern
San Joaquin. In 1852 Alexander McCray
brought 150 to 200 Durham cattle directly from
Indiana: This was a fine line of shorthorn stock.
He grazed his cattle on Kern Island and lived
with his family near the Kern River in an old
adobe house of unknown origin. The oldest
boy, John, roped antelope to add variety to the

family's food supply. There was a shallow hole along the river where oil oozed. Neighbors helped themselves to it to grease machinery. No one thought it had any commercial worth. McCray had it analyzed but was told the substance was valueless.

David Alexander, partner of Phineas Banning, put 20,000 wild Spanish cattle on the San Emigdio hills, around Buena Vista and Kern lakes. These animals roamed into the lower parts of the Kern Delta. Alexander arranged to buy McCray's bull calves to build up the quality of his herd. Thomas Barnes was another cattleman who had brought 40 head and grazed them west of Panama and ran some hogs in the tules. He lived in a large cotton-wood grove that became known as the Barnes settlement.

Mutton was also important to the miners in preventing scurvy. At an early date, possibly as early as 1772, sheep had been driven into the southern San Joaquin Valley because of the fine grazing. Solomon Jewett of Vermont had one of the finest sheep ranches in the United States. His Merino sheep were known internationally. In 1856 his son, Solomon, and John D. Patterson brought the first Merino sheep into the southern San Joaquin by ship and train over the Isthmus of Panama. Later Solomon Jr. brought a herd of Merino sheep across country from Vermont and was joined in the operation by his brother, Philo.

Edward Beale, now a general, also furnished meat to the miners. After he was removed as Indian superintendent, he bought Rancho La Liebre in 1855 in the name of his wife, Mary Edwards Beale. There he raised cattle in partnership with Sam Bishop. The family built a picturesque adobe ranch house there where Beale, his wife Mary, and their son, Truxtun, spent all the time they could.

One interesting episode that concerned both Beale and Fort Tejon had to do with camels. Acting upon a suggestion from Beale, Secretary of War Jefferson Davis ordered the importation of camels into this country in 1857. The army planned to use them in transporting supplies to isolated posts in the arid Southwest and for patrol. A group of 28 camels was marched to Fort Tejon from near San Antonio, Texas. The wagon road survey party to which the camels were attached was under the direction of

Edward Fitzgerald Beale, since by this time, President Buchanan had appointed General Beale to survey a wagon road from Fort Defiance, New Mexico to the Colorado River. For five months, under Beale's care, the camels were a great success. Their splendid performance moved Beale to recommend to the War Department that further camels be purchased. However, most caretakers of the beasts cared nothing for them and seized every opportunity to place them in a poor light. In addition, the rapid expansion of the trans-continental railroads and the outbreak of the Civil War made the American camel corps a short-lived experiment. They were removed to Los Angeles in June 1861.

The first settlers in the southern San Joaquin were attracted by the seemingly endless range and a close market in the nearby gold country. But another advancement helped change this historically renegade part of the West into an area where travel was a little more convenient.

The Butterfield Overland Line or the Great Southern Overland Mail as it was also known, began operations through the southern San Joaquin in October 1858. The valley leg was one segment of a 24-day trip covering 2,888 miles from St. Louis to San Francisco. Headed by John Butterfield, a personal friend of President James Buchanan, the remarkable enterprise was made possible by an annual governmental subsidy of $600,000.

Through the southern San Joaquin, the main vehicle of the line was the celerity wagon. These light vehicles had three seats that would form a bed at night by turning the seat backs down. The body of the wagon was mounted on thoroughbraces instead of steel springs. They traveled day and night and drivers had to have an intimate knowledge of the approximately 60-mile stretch through the valley. A conductor was always seated next to the driver, who had charge of the mail, express, and passengers. Every aspect was regulated by strict rules. But riding on the Overland Stage was a rugged experience and repeat passenger business was very rare.

Although the Butterfield Overland Stage had a short life, as operations ceased by the Civil War era, it accomplished a great deal for the southern San Joaquin. Because of the line, roads had to be much better—for the first time, the

An early photo of a cattle roundup shows a scene typical of the many ranches in Kern County. Courtesy, Kern County Museum

The Jewett Ranch was stocked from the prize flock of Merino sheep that the family had in Vermont. Brought over land and by sea, the Jewetts' sheep were some of Kern County's earliest flocks. Courtesy, Kern County Museum

road from Los Angeles became one of the best mountain roads in the West. The rapid stage, as well as a new telegraph line along its route, made the southern San Joaquin seem less isolated and closer to both San Francisco and Los Angeles and points further east. It contributed to the influx of settlers, especially from the South during and after the Civil War.

But most encouraging for the future town of Bakersfield were the few squatters, who in the early 1860s, settled near the Yokuts village of Woilu. This general area was known as Kern Island. The point of land at the head of the Kern Delta resembled an island and boasted good

soil and plenty of water. Bounded on the east by South Fork, a narrow, steep-banked stream that in general followed the present course of Highway 99, it flowed into Kern Lake (which would have stretched across the present highway). The canal that flows through present-day Central Park is a remnant of the original main channel of the Kern River.

It was here among the Indians on Kern Island that old-timer Thomas Fitzgerald had built his hut to use when hunting. But in February 1860 when Christian Bohna and his large and weary family arrived, the dwelling lay abandoned. After a nine-month journey

from Arkansas, the family gratefully settled in the hut and went to work clearing ten acres of land for corn. Bohna was an educated German, a skilled blacksmith, and well accustomed to frontier life. The family adapted well to the area and the first season netted an impressive 110 bushels of corn per acre. They built a better home amid large cottonwood trees on a small hill south of present-day 24th and P streets. This home was made of cottonwood logs placed upright, woven with tules under a tule roof.

Other settlers soon joined the Bohna family. They settled where they pleased, and if they didn't like the first spot, they tried another. They all cleared land for a garden that was sure to do well. If they were lucky, they had a few cows, hogs, and chickens. As the Indians had done, they built homes out of what was available. The settlers' homes were more permanent than the Indians' had been but less water resistant. There was no lumber, no glass, and no hardware.

Everyone suffered the chills and fever of malaria introduced from Central America in the early part of the century. And there were plenty of other illnesses and injuries to worry about. When young Dr. Sparrel Walter Woody arrived soon after the Bohnas, he must have been given a special welcome. He was a graduate of St. Louis Medical School who had succumbed to gold fever in 1849 and eventually drifted down to Kern Island. He planted corn, potatoes, and grain, and fell in love with Christian's daughter, Sarah Louise. They were married the following year by the visiting circuit preacher. Christian's other daughter, Caroline, married early settler George Brunk, so that made two more families.

Other very early settlers on Kern Island were Robert Gilbert, who farmed near the present site of the Kern County Museum; Walker and John Shirley; the James Harvey Skiles family, who settled west of the Barnes settlement; the Corbin Wicker family; the Lovelace family; James McKenzie; Allen Rose; Jim and Jeff Harris, in the Barnes settlement; and Bill Daugherty in the southern part, a hog raiser and hunter.

Capt. Elisha Stevens had settled on a 38-acre tract east of the present-day Memorial Hospital. He had been a fur trapper, an outstanding emigrant guide, and a Mexican War veteran. He had successfully led a party of pioneers through storms over the Sierra Nevada two years before the Donner party succumbed on the same route. He was now an important member of the Kern Island community, kind and helpful to everyone.

It was a close-knit community, the neighbors, Indian and white alike, helped each other with clearing the land, raising the houses, nursing, and anything else that came up— including disaster. On Christmas Day, 1861, after days of rain, the Skiles family served a feast to the whole settlement. As the Gilbert family returned home afterward, the irrigation ditch that Thomas Barnes had started to dig was filling so rapidly that Mrs. Gilbert, holding her baby, was having difficulty getting across. Some nearby Indians waded into the foamy brown water and carried mother and baby to safety. During the night the water carried away the Gilberts' pig pen, corn crib, and even their house. The current was so strong that the roar of the banks caving in could be heard for miles. When the rains stopped, the river had enlarged and extended Barnes' small canal, diverting the main flow to its present bed.

Truxtun Beale once served as the United States' ambassador to Spain. Beale contributed the well-known clock tower to Bakersfield as a memorial to his mother. The tower stands now at the Kern County Museum. Courtesy, Kern County Museum

Wild grapevines grow along the Kern River and in canyons throughout the valley. Highway 99 over the ridge route got its name "The Grapevine" from these wild vines. Courtesy, Beale Memorial Library; Carlton Watkins Photo

To the white settlers the flood was not entirely ill-omened, for in moving the river to the north and out of the settlement, Kern Island was drier and better for homes. But for the Indians, it was a catastrophe. The constant raining and flooding washed away the small game and fish they depended on. Plus, most of the settlers temporarily moved to the hill at Woilu since it was the driest place. This drove some of the Indians away from the delta; others may have been caught in a government roundup and moved to the Tule River farm along with Indians from the Sebastian Indian Reservation.

The Indians, however, weren't the only ones that left. The Lovelace family and others picked up their belongings and moved. Christian Bohna had had his fill of Kern Island, too. He was lucky. A stranger named Col. Thomas Baker came through and for $200 bought

ground. The Gilberts' new home was on the now-deserted site of Woilu. They lived there only briefly before selling it to Lewis Reeder. Then it became known as Reeder's Hill. But the Reeders had extremely bad luck. Six of the family became mysteriously ill and died. Two others were shot accidentally. Reeder, suffering from tuberculosis and a broken heart, moved to the mountains and died. The house stood empty and forlorn for many years at a place where once a happy and important Indian village had flourished.

On September 10, 1863, the stranger who had bought out Christian Bohna arrived. Colonel Baker; his young wife, Ellen; their daughters, May and Nellie; and son, Thomas, had left Visalia two days earlier. They were the first Kern Island settlers to come from the north. The Bakers moved into the Bohna house. They cleaned and repaired, built a brush shed for a kitchen and dining room, and tacked matting over the vertical cottonwood logs. When they moved in their furniture, considered quite elegant to the collection of squatters, they had the finest home in the community. Capt. Elisha Stevens came soon to welcome the new family bringing them gifts: two hogs, six hens, and a rooster. "I have brought you a start in life," he said simply. The family never forgot that kindness.

But not everyone welcomed the Bakers. To some perhaps it seemed the Bakers had more comforts. But the Bakers were very hospitable people and were not excluded for long. Ellen Baker had the only sewing machine in the settlement, so she invited the other women in to do their fall sewing. Ellen was also concerned about schooling for the children. She opened a school in her own home, inviting the neighbors' children. Having no teaching equipment, she cut letters from paper and used other ingenious devices.

Thus the Bakers gradually were accepted into the little community. This was important to them since they intended to make Kern Island their permanent home. On arriving, Colonel Baker had said, "Here, at last, I have found my resting place; here I expect to lay my bones." For the Bakers had not moved to Kern Island by accident. Their coming was the culmination of a long story, and their presence would have a profound effect on the future of Bakersfield.

Bohna's home and his squatter's rights to 160 acres. Then Christian Bohna and some of his family moved to Oregon. His three married daughters and their husbands moved to the Greenhorn Mountains near the foot of Blue Mountain. There Dr. Woody and Sarah Louise founded the pleasant town of Woody and became ranchers.

But the Shirleys, the Gilberts, the Skiles, and others stayed, rebuilding their homes on higher

The Founders

A THRIVING TOWN IS BORN

This is God's country! Someday it will be filled with happy homes. The largest town south of Stockton will have its site here. Three or four lines of railroads will come through those mountain passes and center here. The place is rich in future possibilities.

—Col. Thomas Baker, 1862, as remembered by his wife, Mrs. Ellen Baker Tracy, The Echo, *1904*

The first Protestant church in Kern County was constructed in Glennville in 1867 and is still in use today. Photo by Gregory Iger

Thomas Baker was born in 1810 to an Ohio family of English origin. They had first settled in Virginia before the American Revolution, then moved to Kentucky, and finally to the Ohio frontier. Young Thomas was interested in both surveying and the law at an early age. While still very young, he was admitted to the Ohio State Bar. At 20 he moved to Illinois and then on to Iowa. Eight years later he was clerk of the district court and a member of the Iowa Territorial Legislative Assembly. He was the first United States district attorney in the territory of Iowa, and a member of its first state legislature. He helped draft the original code and was elected president of the senate, becoming, ex officio, Iowa's first lieutenant governor.

Colonel Baker and his first wife, Mary Featherstone Baker, who was born in London, had four children: William, Nathan David, Eliza, and James. When Colonel Baker was 40 and his children fairly grown, he could no longer resist the Gold Rush. In 1850 he made

his way to Benecia, but soon left for Stockton and the new Tulare County. He built a spacious log home there, but his wife soon passed away. He was co-founder of the town of Visalia and was instrumental in helping it become the county seat. He was elected assemblyman in 1855. Two years later he remarried. His second wife, Ellen Alverson, was only 20 when they married.

During President James Buchanan's administration, Colonel Baker was appointed receiver for the United States Land Office. He was an expert in land law and well versed in the Swamp and Overflow Lands Act of 1857. That authorized the Montgomery brothers, Joseph and William, to reclaim all the state-owned swamp and overflow land between Kings River Slough and Tulare Lake to Buena Vista and Kern lakes. They were also to build a system of navigable canals that would connect Kern, Buena Vista, and Tulare lakes to the San Joaquin River. When these ambitious projects were completed, the Montgomerys would be

Colonel Thomas Baker came to this area when it was nothing but swamp and forest. He worked on reclaiming a large portion of state-owned land which later became Colonel Baker's field, and consequently, Bakersfield. Courtesy, Kern County Museum

awarded all the odd sections of the reclaimed tracts, 200 feet on both sides of the canals, plus the right to the tolls on the canals for 20 years. The entire project was to be completed within four years.

By 1862 five years had gone by and the Montgomerys and their associates had not been able to act. The legislature (of which Colonel Baker was a member) amended the 1857 act, providing an extension of one year on the canals and three years on land reclamation. But the aftermath of the Panic of 1857 had left money scarce. Discouraged, the Montgomery brothers were glad to sell their interests to Colonel Baker and Harvey Brown for $10,000. Other owners sold out for less. Colonel Baker later bought out Brown, but he was no more successful in raising the necessary capital than the Montgomerys had been. The colonel had to ask the legislature for yet another extension and to relieve him of the canal obligation. That was granted in April 1863.

Nature soon stepped in, and perhaps accomplished more toward Colonel Baker's cause than a loan could have done. The help came in the form of a flood in 1867, that diverted the Kern River north of the settlement,

draining much of the swampland. Colonel Baker proceeded to do what he could to make the results of the flood permanent. He hired 30 Indians from the Fort Tejon area and built a headgate on the old South Fork of the Kern River. He also raised a levee that became known as the Town Ditch and built a dam across the northern end of Buena Vista Lake to confine the waters there. His efforts were further benefited by the drought years of 1863-1865, when stock died for lack of range grass and water.

During the Civil War Colonel Baker also devoted his energies to building a better home. The location he chose was later designated as the northwest corner of 19th and N streets in Bakersfield. This house was adobe with a brush roof covered with dirt to give more insulation from the summer heat. Logs were cut in the mountains, floated down the river, and carried by Indian laborers to the site. Mexicans made the adobe bricks. The house was large and snug with huge fireplaces. Its only drawback emerged in rainy weather when black mud dripped from the roof throughout the house until the sun came out and dried things up.

The Baker home was always open to strangers. Their daughter, Charlotte Jameson, recalled: "Colonel Baker and his wife kept open house with true southern hospitality, welcomed every traveler by day or by night, gave him and his family meals, and fed his animals without money or a price being asked or given and found pleasure in doing so; consequently, he died comparatively poor." Colonel Baker even fenced off ten acres of land and planted alfalfa for the use of travelers. That block was approximately bounded by what became M and P streets on the west and east, and 17th and 14th streets on the north and south. This was the only stopping place between Los Angeles and Visalia at the time and it became known as "Baker's field" all along the Los Angeles-Stockton road.

Kern Island was profoundly affected by the Civil War even though conscription was never enforced in California. That was largely due to Gen. Edward F. Beale's recommendation to President Abraham Lincoln that conscription might lose California to the Union. But the southern San Joaquin was settled largely with Southerners and there was considerable

places.

The nearest post office had been at Fort Tejon, but now the mail was left at Visalia and brought by anyone who might be traveling in the general direction of Kern Island. There was no stage line after the Butterfield Overland Mail was discontinued. Thomas A. Baker, Colonel Baker's son, recalled that in 1865,

. . . at the time of [President Abraham] Lincoln's assassination they had received no mail for six weeks and knew nothing of the national sorrow. Then one day a Mexican swam his horse across the river and told them "that the President had been killed." Everyone supposed, naturally enough, that he meant the President of Mexico until some friends in Visalia sent a bundle of newspapers with the news.

No freight wagons were running by this time either, so supplies were scarce. A small mill that Colonel Baker had brought with him to grind grain and corn for the animals was used by the whole community. White flour, if it could be gotten, sold for $10 a sack. But money was even more elusive. Sweet potatoes were dried in ovens and used for coffee. No sugar was available and instead wild honey was gathered from trees along the Kern River. The people found salt deposits and used the salt to cure pork. But every family had a garden that yielded prodigiously.

Several settlers tried to relieve the wartime economic misery by producing cotton, for which the Union was paying well. One of the earliest settlers, James Harvey Skiles, experimented in 1862 with a few acres of cotton south of Reeder Lake. In 1865 Solomon Jewett planted 130 acres of cotton and built a small gin. Jewett's cotton was shipped to the Rector Mills of Alameda County and manufactured into the first cotton material in California.

But Solomon Jewett and his younger brother, Philo, were better known as being the West's outstanding sheep breeders. Wool was also demanding a premium price during the Civil War, especially the fine Merino wool that the Jewetts produced. The southern San Joaquin was rapidly developing into one of the West's great sheep growing areas. During the drought of 1863-1864, the settlers discovered that sheep were much hardier than cattle when the native

Tom Baker, the son of Colonel Thomas Baker, eventually became the sheriff of Bakersfield. Courtesy, Kern County Museum

sympathy for the South. The Los Angeles *Star* urged independence for California. Colonel Baker himself, just a year before he came to Kern Island, had been accused of seditious remarks and held for several days in Camp Babbitt, although he always gave the "most solemn assurances of his loyalty to the General Government." Probably most of the families of Kern Island had members fighting for the Southern cause. Mr. and Mrs. Gilbert each had four brothers enlisted in the Confederate Army.

Strapped for men and money, the Union had to close Fort Tejon during the Civil War. It was a blow to the whole southern valley. There were reports of many secessionists in the area "ready at a moment's warning to take up their arms against the government of the United States." Col. William Jones reported that "a band of robbers and thieves" had made off with property stolen from the government as well as from Union men. Another story told of a band of armed parties camped near Kern Lake. In Panama Slough, a Unionist was attacked by four men "who called themselves Jeff Davis' soldiers." There was great difficulty in keeping the new telegraph line intact from Visalia to Los Angeles. In one day the wire was cut in 12

grass was stunted and the water holes dried up.

Even after the Civil War it took some time for the political waters to cool. Some Californians still hoped that with enough guerilla warfare, California would become an independent Pacific republic. A gang of desperadoes actually formed a plot to this end. Starting from the southern San Joaquin and moving north, they hoped that if they killed every Union man in the valley, the remaining settlers would join in their scheme. The leaders of the gang were John Monroe, alias John Mason, and James Henry, alias Spotty McCauley. They were known as the Mason and Henry Gang, and as the "Bush-whackers," since they would kill a man for any reason. Grizzly Gulch near Woody was one of their hiding places. Once they came down to kill the Jewett brothers at their Rio Bravo sheep ranch because they were known Union sup-porters. Philo Jewett was there with his cook, John Johnson, and a sick Mexican. They did kill Johnson, but Philo and the Mexican escaped.

Colonel Baker was also visited by the mur-derous gang. They were after James Harvey Skiles, a Union man who lived just west of Reeder Hill. Colonel Baker was known to be a Democrat, and the gang wanted him to call Skiles out of his house so they could kill him. Baker, of course, refused to cooperate and even-tually the outlaws left. Then Baker went over to Skiles' house to warn him of the danger, but the gang never showed up in the community again.

As the war tremors waned, a most unusual Southerner appeared briefly in the southern San Joaquin. Asbury Harpending, a young hothead from Kentucky, had already made a fortune mining in Durango, Mexico. With that money he and two other secessionists outfitted a ship with which they hoped to pirate the Pacific Mail liner carrying gold for the Union. The men and the ship were captured, however, and Harpending was convicted of high treason. He was eventually pardoned by President Lin-coln. His friends gave him a horse and some money and advised him "to ride south to . . . the Tulares, where such inhabitants as there were came mostly from the South and where the law writs did not run."

Harpending next turned to prospecting in the Greenhorn Mountains and struck gold in Clear Creek Canyon south of Hot Springs Valley. He laid out the Clear Creek Mining Dis-trict and the townsite of Havilah (named from Genesis, "Havilah, a country rich in gold"). When word of the discovery got out, men flocked into the narrow mountain valley, and Havilah and Harpending prospered noticeably. By selling off his mining claims, the young Southerner banked $800,000 by the end of 1865. Although he soon moved to San Fran-cisco, he continued to take great pride in his town:

Its enterprising inhabitants appeared before the next

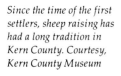

Since the time of the first settlers, sheep raising has had a long tradition in Kern County. Courtesy, Kern County Museum

legislature and asked for the creation of a new county. Though by that time a permanent resident of San Francisco, I assisted in the passage of a bill that cut off from Tulare the county of Kern and named Havilah the county seat . .

And if the matter of paternity is ever brought up in court, it will probably be proven to the satisfaction of a jury that I am the father of Kern County.

Whether or not that claim was valid it is clear that many more people supported the creation of Kern County than had supported Colonel Baker's effort to create Buena Vista County in 1855. A petition for the formation of the new county went around southern Tulare and northern Los Angeles counties. Early in 1866 the 274 signatures collected were sent to Visalia, the Tulare County seat. Resolutions adopted at several meetings in Havilah urged the legislature to authorize the formation of the new county. There was no opposition in the state legislature and Kern County was created on April 2, 1866. Havilah was named as county seat.

The first election in July was quiet, with Henry Hammel, Samuel A. Bishop, and James J. Rhymes elected to the first board of supervisors. Colonel Thomas Baker was named surveyor. In that capacity it was Colonel Baker's responsibility to help set up the county and township boundaries. The first map of the county gives a perfectly perpendicular eastern boundary and a western boundary smoothly following the Coast Ranges. Another matter turned over to Baker was that of swamp and overflow lands. The state recently had turned the administration of the lands over to the counties. Baker had completed his earlier work under the Montgomery franchise. But the area was still in the grip of a severe drought and the drained swamps lay parched and covered with alkali. The board of supervisors was now interested in getting some water back into the area so it could be cultivated. Once again Baker took on the huge job.

His task this time was to construct a levee that would not only turn enough water back into the old South Fork to irrigate the surrounding sands, but would also help to prevent another flood. Water courses would be cleared of timber and growth, and irrigation ditches would run throughout the land. In the Buena Vista area he was to do the same. Baker was to be paid $40,000 for all this work, but since money was virtually nonexistent, he was promised 40,000 acres of land. He had three years, until 1869, to complete the job.

Another assignment for Colonel Baker was to survey a formal townsite. Although there were a number of proposals about just where the town should be, the matter was settled by Gen. William J. Palmer, an engineer with the United States Topographical Corps. Palmer was in the area surveying for a possible extension of the Kansas Pacific Railroad. He recommended a portion of Section 30, specifically the 480 acres bounded by 26th Street on the north, California on the south, H Street on the west, and a line approximately following Kern Island Canal, through Central Park, and down T Street on the east. This was part of the land that Colonel Baker had gained under the Montgomery franchise. But Baker, with his almost consuming vision of a great city, soon sold or gave away all but 80 acres of the land, which he kept for the Baker homestead. Philo Jewett suggested the town be called "Bakersfield" and other community members agreed, especially since it was already generally known as "Baker's field." Colonel Baker planned a civic center (that coincides with the present location) and donated the land for it to the new town.

In 1869 the boundaries of the town contained 17 houses, 2 stores, a blacksmith shop, a livery stable, and a feed stable. Scattered over the whole of Kern Island were perhaps 300 people, including settlers of many origins as well as Indians. The first of the town's two stores was established in a small frame building by the Jewett brothers. Later Julius and George Chester built an adobe store on the corner of 19th Street and Chester Avenue, named in their honor.

But what every new Bakersfield citizen anticipated was the coming of the railroad. The surveying engineer, William Palmer, had reported to Central Pacific officials that passing through Bakersfield was the only logical route between northern and southern California. But it became apparent as early as 1867 that the Central Pacific had concerns that defied logic. In order to finance expansion, the railroads simply bypassed any existing town that refused to provide sizeable land donations. In

In 1871 the intersection of 19th and Chester still had a frontier appearance. Courtesy, Kern County Museum

Bakersfield the railroad wanted two blocks on both sides of the track. Colonel Baker and other town fathers felt that one block on both sides was all the fledgling community could stand.

The little town got a further boost in 1867 when the California governor, Frederick F. Low, sent the surveyor-general and another engineer, Andrew R. Jackson, from Sacramento to examine Colonel Baker's reclamation work on the Montgomery franchise. They agreed that the land was more than adequately drained, and a patent of 89,120 acres of land in Kern and Fresno counties was signed over to Baker on November 11, 1867. The engineer, Andrew Jackson, liked the county so much he stayed and became an active part of Bakersfield developments. Baker soon sold much of the

land to defray costs. Some of it went for 10 cents per acre to as much as $1.50 per acre. Horatio P. Livermore, a wealthy San Francisco druggist, through his agent, Julius Chester, bought large tracts from Colonel Baker.

The five-year drought that had been so helpful to Colonel Baker's land reclamation work finally broke in the fall of 1867. In fact, it rained and rained. Most of the homes had thatched roofs, held in place with dirt on top, and mud floors. The water trickled through washing black water onto the residents' beds, into their food, and onto their floors, creating a pool of mud. The settlers were miserable.

In the mountains, the parched slopes absorbed the rain like a sponge. When thoroughly saturated, trees, slopes, and all crashed down into the steep Kern River Canyon, damming the river. Suddenly down in the delta, the riverbed went dry. On Christmas Eve the river broke through its canyon obstruction and roared out over the delta. The sound of crashing water echoed through the valley, giving the settlers brief warning. Fortunately no lives were lost, but some homes were washed away and many animals drowned.

But, as before, the people made the best of it and were soon building new homes and cleaning up. Huge trees were strewn for ten miles or more down to the Barnes settlement. Thomas Barnes gathered up some logs and built a cabin for his family. Colonel Baker built a sawmill so the townsite could take advantage of the lumber. Unfortunately, when the mill was put to work, sand and stones deeply embedded in the logs ruined the blades, making the mill useless.

But perhaps the saddest result of the flood was that all the swamp and overflow land that Colonel Baker had worked so hard and long to drain, lay under a sheet of water. Some people questioned the value of his work. Others pointed out that Baker's work along the river had considerably lessened the damage to the town. So that there would be no flaws in title to his own property or to the land he had sold or given to the town, Colonel Baker filed an application on December 28, 1868, to purchase from the state all of the land set aside for the town. The application was approved on March 25, 1870.

Undeterred by the flood, Baker took on another challenge to benefit his beloved town. There was no good direct road from the valley to the mountain communities. So he applied for permission to build a toll road from Bena, in the sandy flatlands of Caliente Wash, 12 miles east of Bakersfield, to the Los Angeles-Havilah Road in Walker Basin. This was approved on November 6, 1867, with the stipulation it be fit for practical use on or before the first day of January 1868. The grade was completed within the prescribed time and the road was considered "an engineering marvel." County supervisors fixed the tolls: "for a wagon and two horses, $2.00; for each extra span of horses, 50 cents each; for a horse and rider, 50 cents; for loose animals of all kinds, 25 cents each; for

a footman, 25 cents." This was one of Baker's few paying enterprises and was known as Baker Turnpike, Baker Toll Road, or Baker Grade.

Colonel Baker also set up a gristmill by the stream at the present-day site of the Hill House Motor Inn. General Edward F. Beale had given the set of granite burrs to Colonel Baker and no one was ever charged for using the mill.

A matter of great importance to Colonel Baker and the entire southern San Joaquin was an act adopted by the state legislature that put control of the swamplands back into state control. This canceled Colonel Baker's contract with the county for irrigation ditches and levees on South Fork and around Buena Vista Lake. A very important change in the law removed all restrictions on the amount of land that one individual could buy. The purchaser was required to deposit one dollar per acre with the county treasurer as a guarantee the land would be reclaimed, or a down payment of 20 percent. This was an impossible situation for small farmers, many of whom were squatting on land and couldn't come up with the cash. Some of them became discouraged and left, knowing their land was open for purchase unless they could produce the money.

Nevertheless, by early 1869 the demand for Kern County land was increasing, and Colonel Baker established a real estate office in Bakersfield. He again ran for state senator as an independent that summer. The *Tulare Times*, however, brought up the old, unproven 1862

This 1900s photo shows Havilah, an early county seat of Kern County. The town boomed during the gold-mining era and slowly declined as the agricultural community of Bakersfield grew. In its heyday the population was over 3,000, but today only a handful of people live there. Courtesy, Ticor

charges of sedition against Colonel Baker, and he was defeated. But, he still had plenty to do in Bakersfield and Kern County.

By 1869 it was becoming clear that the population of Bakersfield was steadily growing, while that of Havilah was shrinking. Augustus D. Jones, editor of the *Havilah Courier*, told of his "Trip to the Island," where he found the stores of Chester & Company, Cohn, Jacoby and Company, and a church. The first public school had just been built. It was a 40-by-60-foot brick building, between G and H streets on California Avenue. Former state engineer Andrew Jackson was the teacher of 35 pupils. Bakersfield even had a "fire department," so to speak. Colonel Baker hung an iron rim from a wagon wheel on a tree and placed a sledge-hammer nearby on the corner of 19th and M streets. Beside it he maintained a wagon loaded with barrels of water and wooden buckets. In addition a saloon was being built, and a photograph gallery and blacksmith shop would soon be ready for business.

On December 14, 1869, Havilah newspaper owner Augustus D. Jones announced that he and his paper were moving to Bakersfield, and Havilah subscribers could receive the paper from its new home. It continued without missing an issue as the *Kern County Courier*.

A few months later Jones had a chance to sell the newspaper, and he did. Julius Chester bought it with Horatio P. Livermore's money. Richard Hudnut, one of the founding fathers of Kernville, became the editor, and the politics of the paper made a complete turnabout: the one newspaper of the area was now Republican.

Bakersfield was beginning to show an embryonic prosperity. The fertility of the area and the hard work of its citizens were starting to bring money in. The sheep men were quite successful: the Jewett brothers, Daniel Troy, Gustave Sanger, Gen. Edward F. Beale, Robert Baker, and others. The cattle of Ferdinand A. Tracy, Wellington Canfield, George Young, and William Landers made substantial contributions. In addition the townspeople sold horses, mules, lumber, and posts. And money still came in from gold in the Greenhorn Mountains.

Colonel Baker had resurveyed the city in 1869. A lithographed map was made and filed with the county recorder. Oddly enough, on

December 14, 1870, William J. Yoakum, who lived on the town property he had bought from Colonel Baker, made application for the whole of section 30 as swampland (hoping to lay claim to the townsite simply by filing for the land and draining it), but the state surveyor general did not approve it.

By the spring of 1871 prosperity and a permanent population of around 600 scored another Bakersfield first when the Bakersfield Club was formed. This was an important step as it was the forerunner of the Bakersfield Chamber of Commerce and evidence of the necessary cohesiveness for successful town development. Other organizations soon followed. The Kern County Agricultural Society stated its purpose as "making agriculture the leading interest of the county."

The California Cotton Growers and Manufacturer's Association was organized in August 1871. It purchased 10,000 acres at $5.00 per acre from Livermore and Chester. The founders envisioned creating a "vast plantation . . . divided into cotton parks of 50 to 100 acres each." Members hoped to engage in as many other industries as might "be kindred to and spring out of the main enterprise." Their prospectus claimed ownership of the townsite of Bakersfield, 16 houses, a large brick store and warehouse, the power and privileges of the Kern Island Irrigation Company's canal, the merchandising and transportation of Livermore & Chester, an improved farm with tools, teams, and other equipment, and the *Kern County Weekly Courier*. The firm stated it was composed of "Californians and Englishmen" who had studied all of the San Joaquin Valley and had chosen the Kern Delta for their operations. The president was Louis H. Bonestell, and the secretary, James D. Johnston. A promotional campaign followed to interest other investors.

Plans were made to plant 1,000 acres to cotton in the spring of 1872, under the supervision of William G. Allen. Chinese laborers were hired but neither the investors nor the workers knew enough about proper irrigation. By fall expenses had far exceeded the prospects of income. John H. Redington, a San Francisco business associate of Livermore's, who became trustee, found matters badly mismanaged. Julius Chester was discharged

from the California Cotton Growers and Manufacturer's Association, and it took some time to untangle the accounts. In sorting out the losses, Chester's brother, George, received the general merchandise store, Richard Hudnut became owner of the *Courier*, Livermore kept his interest in the Kern River Flour Mill that had just been started, and Redington and Livermore received control of the unsold land. The association was subsequently dissolved.

In the meantime Bakersfield's travel connections had improved when the Telegraph Stage Company included Bakersfield on its runs from Los Angeles to the end of the Southern Pacific in Fresno. The Southern Pacific surveyors laid out their rail line in Kern County and it was clear they were going to miss Bakersfield. This was a disappointment, but the residents of Bakersfield felt fiercely loyal to their town and continued to build. The Southern Pacific's depot was a mile and a half to the east of Sumner.

Colonel Baker, Andrew R. Jackson, and Morris Jacoby had earlier formed a committee to put up a town hall. The lower floor was to be used for social and theatrical purposes and the upper floor as a meeting hall. A public subscription quickly raised $3,200 so the hall could be ready for a Christmas ball in 1871, which was well attended.

The final touches were put on the Town Hall in 1872 and it sparked a new wave of organizational activity. Kern Lodge, Number 202, Independent Order of Odd Fellows, started meeting on the upper floor. A number of religious groups, the Methodists for one, held Sunday services in the Town Hall. The beginnings of the Catholic Church had been laid earlier. The first Mass in Bakersfield was held in October 1871 in the rear of Paul Galtes' store on 19th Street between Chester

and K Street. A number of Chinese had come to Bakersfield from mining camps, local railroad construction, and as agricultural labor. Their first temple was built in the early 1870s in the middle of a strawberry patch near Colonel Baker's mill.

The town now had three saloons, and a brewery run by Henry A. Jastro, Colonel Baker's son-in-law. A hotel association was formed and plans were made to sell stock to build a "first class hostelry." A well-known architect, Hugh McKeadney, drew up plans for a three-story building that would cost roughly $20,000.

The greatest threat to the new structures was always fire. In 1872 a building owned by Constantine Baker, used as a bakery, restaurant, and barber shop, burned to the ground. The answer to flammability was to use brick as building material. But no one yet had been able to fire bricks in the area. Colonel Baker was finally successful and he promised bricks would soon be available. But he never lived to see it.

About that time an epidemic of typhoid broke out in Bakersfield, and Colonel Baker fell victim. Mrs. Baker's father, Dr. Labon Alverson, who had moved to Tehachapi, came to attend the ailing man, but Baker soon developed pneumonia. He only lasted a few days, then passed away peacefully in his sleep on November 24, 1872. Practically the whole town attended Colonel Baker's funeral held in the Town Hall he had instigated. His funeral service was conducted by the Masonic Order from Visalia, which he had helped organize in 1852. And he was buried in Union Cemetery, which he had laid out. His prophecy that he would lay his bones in Kern Delta was fulfilled, and in just ten years, his vision had given his namesake town a sturdy foundation.

Southern Pacific's "El Gobernador" was one of the fastest engines on the Bakersfield line in the 1880s.

The Warriors

BATTLE FOR THE KERN

The history of Bakersfield is a story of hope deferred, of promises unfulfilled. First we prayed for a railroad. We got it, but it did not unlock the door of our possibilities as we expected it would. Then we prayed for colonization. Everything was made ready to answer that prayer, when the contest over water rights interfered and nothing could be done toward cutting up the land until that was settled. When it was out of the way and the colonization scheme was undertaken, just at the start, when everybody's hope was stimulated, the town burned up.

—Wallace M. Morgan, History of Kern County, 1914

The Kern River railroad bridge is pictured here under construction in the 1870s. The bridge added another link between Bakersfield and the rest of the state.

Within six months of Col. Thomas Baker's death, almost every citizen had signed a petition requesting incorporation of the little town of Bakersfield. Elections for town officials were held May 24, 1873. According to author Charles Nordoff, Bakersfield in 1873 still had a "decidedly frontier look," and the new town officials found plenty to do. They began by establishing ordinances and fees: a tax of $20 for general merchandise stores, $10 for breweries, and less for other businesses. It became illegal to drive a horse or mule faster than six miles an hour within town limits. They stipulated that bridges over the canals must be the same width as streets. No more than three cubic feet of litter could be piled on business streets. Using water from the ditches without permission became petty larceny, and bathing in the ditches was forbidden. The politicians hoped these steps would encourage order in the flourishing village.

A further step forward in the business community was the establishment of Masonic Lodge Number 224, Free and Accepted Masons. It was called a "moonlight lodge" because its monthly meetings were held on Thursdays before full moons to enable members to ride home by moonlight. The meetings were held in the Town Hall, shared with Kern Lodge Number 202, Independent Order of Odd Fellows, organized the year before. Both organizations were important to the development of the town and included most of the leading citizens.

Another very early Bakersfield organization was the National Grange of the Patrons of Husbandry. The group's avowed purpose was to improve conditions for small farmers who were beginning to move into the rich, sparsely populated Kern Delta. The Kern County

This group photo at the Alameda Farm includes (left) Mrs. Alex Mills, Mrs. N.E. Houghton, Bessie Houghton, S.W. Wible, Mrs. Moulty, Mrs. George Price, Hugh Metcalf, Miss Metcalf, and Mr. James (Alameda farm superintendent). Courtesy, Beale Memorial Library; Carlton Watkins Photo

Agricultural Society estimated there were 555,460 acres of first-class agricultural land, but only about a fourth, or 120,000 acres, belonged to the government and was available to home-steaders. Half of that land was already in the hands of a few large landholders. The other quarter was reserved for the Southern Pacific Railroad, pending confirmation of its land grant. Even so, the Agricultural Society felt there was room for at least 5,800 home-stead families, or, they said, a population of 58,000. (Families were expected to be large in those days.)

The prospect of a large farm population, however, infuriated the cattle ranchers. The valley had always been one huge, unfenced pasture with thousands of freely roaming cattle. But these herds made homesteading impossible, breaking through farmers' fences, consuming crops, and even knocking down homestead shanties, endangering the women and children. The farmers prevailed in 1874 when a law was passed requiring that livestock

be fenced. But this was only the first step toward opening the region to agriculture.

The next challenge was to transform the Kern Delta from lake, swamp, and prairie into American-style farmland. This required drainage in many areas, then the construction of irrigation canals. When settlers began to come in earnest in 1873, not even 5,000 acres were irrigated. The existing canals and ditches had all been laboriously dug by hand with shovels, small plows, and scrapers. But William H. Souther, the superintendent of the 10,000-acre Kern River ranch of San Franciscans Horatio P. Livermore and John H. Redington, hoped to be more efficient. He designed and built a three-ton plow that would cut a furrow eight feet wide and six feet deep. It took 80 oxen to move the unwieldy device guided by one unfortunate man in the rear. But the furrow would turn properly only when the oxen were running and this was virtually impossible to accomplish. So Souther ditched the giant plow and fashioned a smaller one to be pulled by

40 mules. This plow scoured well with the faster animals and was used to finish the Kern Island canals.

The owners of the ranch that Souther supervised, Livermore and Redington, managed an international wholesale drug firm from their San Francisco base. These wealthy landowners wanted to divide their ranch into small farms and sell them to homesteaders. The people of Bakersfield heartily approved of this plan. But before the necessary settlers would come, the region needed a cheap means of moving farm produce to San Francisco and other markets. The answer to this problem, everyone agreed, was the long-anticipated railroad, which was now making its way down the valley.

The Central Pacific, as usual, was making the most of its government land grants. Towns not meeting railroad demands were bypassed and a new town was laid out on railroad land.

The first to be bypassed was Stockton, the hub of the northern valley. A new Central Pacific town named Lathrop was established one mile east of the San Joaquin River. Then Modesto, Merced, and Fresno were all laid out on railroad land. But when the railroad laid out Tulare eight miles east of Visalia, Bakersfield

residents became worried. They wanted the rail to come through their town but still had no intention of complying with the railroad's demand for two full blocks on both sides of the route through town. Besides, the people couldn't believe the Central Pacific would ignore the advice of their own investigator who had called Bakersfield the logical rail center for the southern San Joaquin Valley.

To cover the franchise and land grants beyond Visalia, the Central Pacific had acquired the Southern Pacific line. In the summer of

Top: Owned by the Pioneer Canal Company, the Pioneer Canal was used to redirect Kern River water to other areas. Courtesy, Beale Memorial Library; Carlton Watkins Photo

Above: The world's largest animal-drawn plow was designed to dig canals by W.G. Souther.

47

1873, now under the name of Southern Pacific, the same work crews—mostly Chinese—pushed the rails rapidly south from Tulare and Goshen across the Kern County line. A town established barely within the county was called Elno at first. But after United States Secretary of the Interior Columbus Delano arranged for Southern Pacific ownership of the town, it was renamed Delano.

Delano remained the end of the rail line for 11 months, as the Southern Pacific suffered in the throes of the national depression of 1873. During this time the new town sprouted, quickly becoming a busy rail terminal. All freight coming and going to the southern San Joaquin now went through Delano.

Early in 1874 Bakersfield residents thought their long wait for the iron rails was nearly over when a group of distinguished gentlemen visited from San Francisco. The most impressive was Leland Stanford, the former governor of California, vice-president of Southern Pacific, and president of Central Pacific. With him were about ten other railroad officials, bankers, and political figures. Editor Richard Hudnut of the *Kern County Weekly Courier* reported that in a three-hour conversation with these men, Leland Stanford assured him that Bakersfield was the most important town on the line, and that the Southern Pacific would not dream of bypassing it.

On April 6, 1874, the rails finally started moving south from Delano as crews laid down a half mile of track a day. Four months later they reached the north bank of the Kern River. Here a temporary station, Mesa, was used while the railroad bridge was built over the river. The *Courier* happily reported, "From the town we can hear locomotive whistles. And for all practical purposes the railroad has reached Bakersfield."

Loads of Oregon fir were freighted down to build the bridge. Logs were driven into the Kern River bed with steam pile drivers. It took two months for a sturdy bridge to be constructed. In ten more days a little funnel-stacked locomotive was chugging over the Kern River and going as far as Chester Avenue near the old ice house. This was a busy, prosperous time for little Bakersfield with abundant business and new stores and homes going up. Adding to the excitement was the

erection of a new county building.

As early as 1871 the Bakersfield Club, forerunner of the Bakersfield Chamber of Commerce, had backed moving the county seat from Havilah to Bakersfield. A petition to make the transfer was successfully circulated by 1872, while Colonel Baker was still alive. It had been approved by the state legislature, but the governor did not sign the bill. A new code, however, was passed, requiring the county board of supervisors to call an election if two-thirds of the county requested it. The necessary signatures were collected and one of the supervisors, Solomon Jewett, made sure an election to determine the county seat location was called.

When the final tally of the 1873 election was in, Bakersfield had won by eight votes. But this result was contested by supervisors from Havilah and Tehachapi, who declared some votes were invalid. It took almost a year of protracted legal battling before the winner was determined. Judge Alexander Deering of Visalia finally ordered that all votes were valid and declared Bakersfield the county seat in January 1874. At long last the town could be triumphant. On January 31, 1874 county officials were welcomed at a ball in the Town Hall hosted by the Odd Fellows and Masons. This was followed by a dinner at the elegant, newly built French Hotel.

The town's jubilation was quickly converted into action. George Chester donated a block of land just south of Truxtun on Chester Avenue (the present site of the Bakersfield City Hall) for the new county courthouse. Plans were drawn by architect Albert Bennett, and a bid of $29,999 accepted from Oakland builder Alfred Burrell. Still it would take two years for the handsome structure to be completed.

Winning the county seat was about the only consolation for Bakersfield residents when it became apparent that the railroad was not coming to town, as Leland Stanford had "promised." Chester Avenue had been the end of the line for only a few weeks when in the fall of 1874 Chinese laborers resumed work. The town watched in dismay as the track went a mile and a half to the east into an "entirely uninhabited plain of treeless, waterless, and barren soil," as the *Courier* bitterly described it.

There, in October 1874, the first passenger-

Opposite top: The Kern Island Canal, in this Carlton Watkins photo, was one of the primary canals that carried water to irrigate local farms. Courtesy, Beale Memorial Library

Opposite below: Delano was the first Southern Pacific Railroad town in Kern County, and as such it enjoyed several years of prosperity. Courtesy, Ticor

Kern County officials sat on the Court House steps for this 1885 photo. Seated: Wm. Tyler, county auditor; Wm. Bower, sheriff; N. Van Orman, deputy sheriff; Dave Sinclair, jailer; Zip Cuons, undersheriff. Standing: Thomas Harding, assessor; Gene Freeman, district attorney; N.R. Packard, county clerk; R.E. Arick, judge, Superior Court; A.P. Bernard, county treasurer; W.A. Howell, official court reporter. Courtesy, Beale Memorial Library

freight train pulled to a stop beside a makeshift building that passed as a railway depot. A sign announcing "Sumner" was erected, in honor of Charles Sumner, a U.S. senator from Massachusetts. Soon a town was laid out by Southern Pacific officials with lots measuring 24-by-150 feet. Temporary shacks were rapidly erected to meet immediate needs at the new end of the line.

The people of Bakersfield were momentarily stunned. An unpopular suggestion was made to change Bakersfield's name to Sumner, and a few predicted that many businesses would move to the rival town with the railroad station. The new *Kern County Gazette* moved to Sumner on the invitation of the merchants there, but moved back to Bakersfield within a year. On the whole the townspeople felt that Bakersfield was in the right place; it was the railroad station that was misplaced.

In any case the shock was short-lived and Bakersfield residents quickly arranged for

connections with Sumner. A telegraph line and several horse-drawn omnibus services soon provided links. Bakersfield had the best accommodations in the area, so many new arrivals hurried there; and every business was crowded and busy.

As before, the Southern Pacific didn't stop to discuss local problems. They continued laying track toward the difficult and steep Tehachapi Pass, near which Southern Pacific set up a work depot named Caliente. Most everyone believed Caliente would remain the end of the line. The small post-Civil War trains could climb grades of no more than 2.2 percent and ahead lay a 3,000-foot climb in only 16 miles.

But Chief Engineer William Hood had his own ideas. Instead of starting at Caliente where the real climb began, he followed the contour of the slope curving slowly down. At the famous "Tehachapi Loop," considered the outstanding engineering accomplishment of early railroad history, he laid out a complete circle that passed

under itself, 3,794 feet in radius. By this means, the train could keep to the 2.2 percent grade.

When construction began in earnest, blasting consumed 600 barrels of black powder daily. More than 12,000 men cut, dug, filled, carted, and dumped at top speed. Eighteen tunnels, 22 feet high and 16 feet wide were braced with 14-inch redwood. It was hard, dangerous work, and casualties from tunnel cave-ins, premature blasts, and other mishaps were "so frequent that they no longer attract attention and are looked upon as a matter of course," commented the *Courier*. More than 300 Chinese laborers were killed in laying the road to Tehachapi.

Having conquered the Tehachapi grade, the Southern Pacific track proceeded quickly to Mojave. By August tracklaying in Kern County was complete. The rail line had simultaneously been laid north from Los Angeles, and the two portions were joined at Lang in Soledad Canyon, where the spike ceremony took place in September 1876.

Bakersfield and Kern County were on a continuous rail line that would soon have two transcontinental connections, one to the south as well as to the north. At last people and produce could be taken quickly anywhere in the country. The fertile, well-watered Kern Delta was no longer isolated behind mountains on three sides and the long trip down the San Joaquin Valley by horse and wagon or stage.

Bakersfield had watched in fascination as the railroad made its way over Tehachapi Pass. But there was also progress to admire at home. The wonderful new courthouse was completed, and its formal acceptance was celebrated in April 1876. It was regarded as one of the finest courthouses in the state for many years. Great

pride was taken in the two-acre grounds that eventually featured pleasant walks through a collection of trees and shrubs. It was all surrounded by an elegant white wood fence.

But perhaps the old County Courthouse grounds were more remembered for six bodies that hung from a heavy timber between two native willow trees. The men had been accused of stealing horses from a Bakersfield livery stable and other offenses in Kern County. A posse captured and brought the renegades back to the county jail. The captors immediately named their own court officials and held a trial. The defense lost and all six captives were summarily hanged on December 15, 1877. The stiff bodies hanging in the courthouse yard served as a grisly reminder for any would-be horse thieves.

The people of Bakersfield were equally efficient in April 1876 when criticism was mounting against the town government. Rumor had it that the main problem was the town marshal, Alex Mills. Mills was a Kentuckian who had lost a leg in the Civil War, but he was a sure shot. It was said that he would enter a business and, if money due the town was not handed over immediately, he would shoot holes in the floor around the proprietor's feet. City officials decided to fire Mills, but word came back that Mills would retaliate with his very accurate shotgun.

Bakersfield trustee president Henry A. Jastro offered a solution: disincorporate the town and so do away with the position of town marshal. A petition was signed by 69 residents, and the disincorporation was approved by the Kern County Board of Supervisors. Bakersfield no longer had to pay $76 a month to Alex Mills.

Throughout the decade, incorporated or not,

Before the turn of the century, other towns were more prominent than Bakersfield in Kern County. The main street of Tehachapi, one of those towns, is pictured here from the 1880s. Courtesy, Ticor

new buildings sprouted. A new, white shiplap structure for the Kern Valley Bank was built on the southwest corner of Chester and 18th streets. Nineteenth and Chester was still the business center of the town. One of many new additions was the fine new Arlington House on the southeast corner, a large two-story board and batten hotel. The second floor opened onto a balcony with no railing. When the cowboys came to town on Saturday nights for a little fun, it was fair sport to lasso anyone or anything from this balcony.

But the cowboys were not solely responsible for Bakersfield's reputation as a lively town in the 1870s. The Town Hall was now freed from official county functions. Available for meetings and celebrations, it was a scene of many good times. The volunteer firemen were the social lions among the young set. It was the particular delight of the Alert Hook and Ladder Company to make their entry through the upstairs windows of the Town Hall when a dance was in full swing. On special occasions even more energetic celebrations took place. Mexican Independence days were marked by bear and bullfights, a delight to most of the population—and the Fourth of July by fireworks, parades, and picnics. Baseball was already a popular sport and Bakersfield's

The members of the Alert Hook and Ladder Company, posed in front of the Kern Valley Bank, were known for their conviviality as much as for their firefighting ability. Courtesy, Kern County Museum

The Arlington Hotel was one of Bakersfield's popular hostelries in the late 19th century. Courtesy, Kern County Museum

winning team was known as the "Two Orphans." They played the Visalia Empire Club twice in 1879, and beat them both times. (Of 102 runs scored, the Two Orphans earned 75.)

Despite the good times there was always the fear of fire. The town finally built a real fire station in the spring of 1877. The first Bakersfield fire station, a small, one-story wooden building opposite the French Hotel, housed a hook and ladder truck, a wagon equipped with six fire extinguishers, several leather buckets, some short ladders, and a few axes. By 1877 it also had a hand-powered fire engine as well as several hose carts. Even with this new equipment, however, the year 1877 alone saw the demise in flames of the Old Stage Hotel, then Jastro's brewery, and the new Railroad Avenue School on Truxtun.

Compounding the hazards of these fires was a drought hanging heavy over Kern Delta in 1877. Very little rain had fallen and the river

was low in its banks. Bakersfield residents chose this ideal time to erect a long-overdue bridge across the Kern. It was decided to put the town bridge down Jewett Lane, so the main road out of town went past the Jewett farm. But that year of terrible drought brought on the biggest water war ever waged in Kern County.

The range, in 1877, was brown and sparse, and only those ranches with enough irrigated alfalfa land were able to take care of their sheep and cattle. North of the delta, San Franciscans Livermore and Redington owned the 10,000-acre Kern River ranch, which was irrigated by their own Kern Valley Water Company. Downstream, "Boss" Billy Carr—a powerful Republican and manipulator for the Southern Pacific Railroad—had acquired the 59,434 Gates tract in the heart of the Kern River Delta for James Ben Ali Haggin and Lloyd Tevis, one of the most aggressive and successful investment partnerships on the Pacific Coast.

Lloyd Tevis was a San Francisco banker, a

Another document from Carlton Watkins' trips to Kern County is this photo of the superintendent's home at the Poso Ranch. The ranch covered more than 20,000 acres with most of the land planted in alfalfa. Courtesy, Beale Memorial Library

Buena Vista Ranch, covering 18,000 acres, was one of the large ranches photographed by Carlton Watkins to document Kern County's agricultural richness. Pictured here are the haymakers on their way to harvest alfalfa. Courtesy, Beale Memorial Library

president of Wells Fargo and Co., and a vice-president of Southern Pacific. James Ben Ali Haggin was the shrewd investor. They were also partners in mining ventures with George Hearst. Together they owned the greatest silver mine, the *Ontario;* the greatest gold mine, the *Homestake;* and the greatest copper mine, the *Anaconda.* Money from these mines and other profitable ventures financed Billy Carr in Kern County. Tevis and Haggin apparently gave Carr discretionary power in purchases and improvements in building up their Kern County empire. Billy Carr was a new kind of political force in Kern County. A big forceful man with great charm and persuasiveness, "Boss" Carr had seemingly unlimited funds behind him. He envisioned that with irrigation the Kern Delta would become "the garden of the earth." All he needed to accomplish this was absolute control of the Kern River and ownership of most of the land. He felt justified in using any means to accomplish this end.

Since the Carr-Haggin-Tevis land did not front on the Kern River, Carr encouraged farmers to put in their own irrigation canals, providing financial backing in return for 51 percent of the stock in the water company.

Henry Miller and Charles Lux owned the lowest part of the Kern River and Delta, all the land between Buena Vista and Tulare lakes. They were wholesale meat producers and retailers, and owned their own rangeland, as well as the land used to drive the cattle to the San Francisco market.

Up to this time there were no laws governing the distribution of water, and each user took water out of the Kern River according to his need. But in this dry year Livermore and Redington built a $20,000 dam using boulders, gravel, and timbers at their Kern Island takeoff. Farmers below the dam were concerned that water would be cut off, so Carr got a restraining order on any further construction of the dam. But work continued until the Kern Island dam was mysteriously dynamited. The culprit or culprits remain unknown to this day.

Livermore and Redington, however, went ahead with their plans to divide their 10,000-acre ranch into small farms and even printed a book with pictures and maps promoting it. But before they were able to sell the small parcels, Haggin, Tevis, and Carr bought the whole colony. Even though Livermore and Redington owned one of the largest wholesale drug companies in the United States, they apparently recognized that they were no match for Haggin and Tevis, who had mineral, banking, and other business interests all over the world.

Central to the developing controversy was the largest canal yet conceived, which in 1876 was started on the north side of the Kern River by Oliver P. Calloway, a San Francisco engineer. His dream was to irrigate 35,000 acres, financed by selling the land for $14 an

The Jackson Ranch was the setting for this Carlton Watkins photo of workers opening the sluice to irrigate alfalfa fields. Courtesy, Beale Memorial Library

Henry Miller, of Miller and Lux Cattle, was a plaintiff in an early water rights dispute over Kern River water. The resulting compromise set the precedent for future water allocation. Courtesy, George Nickel

acre, with each purchaser also buying $2,000 worth of stock in the Kern River Land & Canal Company. Although Calloway ran into problems in purchasing the land from both the railroad and the government, he began the 100-foot wide canal. But only three miles were completed for, without clear title to the land, it was impossible to get financing.

The settlers and farmers in Bakersfield were unaware that Congress in the meantime had passed the Desert Land Act on March 3, 1877. Chief sponsor of the bill was Billy Carr's friend, Senator Aaron A. Sargent of California. Under this act any citizen could file a claim on land that couldn't sustain a crop without irrigation. By paying 25 cents per acre at the time of filing, the applicant had three years to provide water to the land; then an additional dollar an acre secured the deed. Somehow Billy Carr knew about the Desert Land Act long before anyone else. His efforts to acquire the whole body of "desert" land north of Kern River and even on Kern Island (anything but arid) became one of the last scandals of President Ulysses S. Grant's administration.

Carr had filed proxy applications at the Visalia Land Office several days before news of the new act arrived. The clerks there were instructed to record these applications over the weekend before anyone else had a chance to file. This produced such an outcry throughout California, most notably in the *San Francisco Chronicle*, that both houses of the state legislature passed a resolution asking Congress to repeal the Desert Land Act. Carl Schurz, who was Secretary of the Interior under President Rutherford Hayes, ordered all of Carr's entries suspended and sent an investigator into the area (to Visalia). A trial followed in which Haggin himself testified that he regretted the money he had spent on the Kern River lands. But he also insisted he would stay with the project until the land could be divided up into small tracts with water rights for the tracts' owners.

Although the government land titles remained in suspension, Carr, Haggin, and Tevis quickly bought up the railroad land, which through connections was readily available to them, and proceeded with the Calloway Canal. It took Carr about a year to complete the remaining 25 miles. When the

canal was ready for use in 1879, it worked remarkably well: so well, in fact, it diverted the entire Kern River northward up the Calloway Canal.

Downstream farms and the sloughs were left high and dry. Cowboys and farmers alike retaliated by tearing out the new weir, hoping to get some water to save their crops and stock. Sometimes shots were exchanged. The strong opinions of the residents on the water issue were echoed in the press. Julius Chester, who founded the *Southern Californian*, became a strong advocate of downstream landowners Henry Miller and Charles Lux. Richard Hudnut, who edited the *Kern County Californian*, supported the water claims of Haggin and Carr. Many local people felt there was a third interest—that of the people themselves. To reflect the view that the state should regulate the water in trust for the people, farmers and businessmen established the *Kern County Echo*, edited by a young lawyer, Sylvester C. Smith.

Miller, Lux, and others with downstream interests filed a lawsuit against the upstream appropriators. The trial began in the Kern County Superior Court in April 1881 under

The Mountain View Dairy had a herd of 175 cows at the time of this Carlton Watkins photo. Courtesy, Beale Memorial Library

Below: Pictured here is the curing room of the Kern Island Dairy, a large cheesemaking business. Courtesy, Beale Memorial Library; Carlton Watkins Photo

Bottom: Hops, used in brewing beer, were an unusual crop in Bakersfield. Finding stock and alfalfa raising more profitable, the "Hop Ranch" ultimately returned to those endeavors.

Judge Benjamin Brundage. Known nationwide as *Lux* vs. *Haggin*, the trial made good newspaper copy not only because it involved two of the wealthiest and most successful partnerships on the West Coast, but also because it dealt with water issues critical to the development of the arid states.

Two principles were at odds in the web of conflicting claims. Miller and Lux said the Kern water belonged to them because they owned the land on the natural river course. This idea of riparian rights, based on early American law, had been written into the California constitution in 1850. Haggin, Tevis, and Carr, who had diverted the Kern River in order to irrigate vast tracts of their own land, maintained they were appropriating the water to the greater good. (The principle of appropriation had also been accepted in California since the Gold Rush.)

The trial lasted for 45 days, but on November 3, Judge Brundage ruled in favor of Haggin and Tevis. Miller and Lux appealed to the state Supreme Court, which made a decision on October 27, 1884. But the decision was not filed in Bakersfield until May 28, 1886: the justices, in one of the longest opinions in California history, had decided in favor of Miller and Lux.

It was not, however, in anyone's best interest to return the Kern River to its natural course. The solution finally came in the form of a compromise proposed by Henry Miller. Kern River water would be measured above Gordon's Ferry, and a third of it—during

Independence Day in 1892 was a festive day celebrated with the usual parade. Philip Niederaur sits with his decorated horse and buggy waiting to take part in the procession. Courtesy, Kern County Museum

March, April, May, June, July, and August—would belong to Miller and Lux. Haggin and Tevis and the canal companies would get the rest and, in return, would assist in constructing a reservoir out of Buena Vista Lake for Miller and Lux. This agreement was signed on July 28, 1888, by 31 corporations and 58 individuals.

By now Haggin and Tevis owned more than 400,000 acres south and north of the Kern River. Even though their title to the Desert Land Act land was still in suspension, Carr proceeded with his dream of developing the best irrigation system in the world. Generously using Haggin's and Tevis' money, as well as his own, 14 huge ranches were developed, the corporate farms of their day. The main business on the ranches was still cattle, but there was some farming, and alfalfa was the leading crop. The herds were gathered in the spring at the Livermore ranch bordering Kern and Buena Vista lakes, and were driven by the vaqueros to

the San Emigdio Ranch where they ranged the mountains until the fall roundup.

For many people in Bakersfield—particularly the settlers and small farmers—these same years were hard times. The population of Kern County from 1880 to 1886 had stood still, while Fresno County increased by 89 percent and Tulare by 66 percent. Schools were shut down as homesteaders lost hope of ever gaining title to their land.

Bakersfield itself remained a dusty, Western cow-and-sheep town, a town that was dealt a further blow on June 2, 1883, when a terrible fire broke out downtown from a coal oil lamp explosion. The Bakersfield Fire Department rushed to the rescue, but was ineffective because the water supply was so low. The fire spread rapidly from building to building. Goods were piled in the street in hopes of saving them from the burning buildings. But anything that the fire didn't consume, thieves

took. A loss of $35,000 was estimated.

For several years this was referred to as "the big fire," and it would have been bigger had there been a breeze. Plans were made to protect the town with a better water supply, and by November 1883 the Bakersfield Water Works had started operation. Three 60-foot wells were drilled on the southeast corner of 17th Street and Chester Avenue. Nearby a small building protected a steam engine that ran a pump to raise the water up to the 80-foot tank housed in an attractive tower. This was designed to send 15,000 gallons of water per hour through a network of four-inch cedar conduits to cisterns sunk under the main street intersections. The people of Bakersfield felt much more secure with this "modern" fire protection system.

A breakthrough for the town finally came when the water agreement between Haggin and Tevis and Miller and Lux was signed on July 28, 1888. Everyone was relieved and hopeful that Haggin and Tevis would subdivide and sell their extensive holdings as soon as possible. And true to Haggin's statements, the first properties were soon offered for sale. An auction was held December 17, 1888, and in two hours 92 lots were sold. Within five days, 19 colony lots of five acres each were sold as well as 145 town lots. Town parcels sold for $100 to $640 and other land at $35 to $57 an acre.

This development opened a floodgate of progress as a new era of enthusiasm and enterprise dawned in Bakersfield. The Bakersfield and Sumner Street Railway was laid and began operation with little 12-seat cars pulled down the track by mules. Another innovation was the Bakersfield Telephone Exchange, established on October 1, 1888, with 29 businesses and residences on the line. And Bakersfield Gas Works opened, furnishing the marvel of gaslight to 52 customers.

The optimism also sparked a new wave of construction. The Southern Hotel Association built a fine new brick hotel on the northwest corner of 19th Street and Chester Avenue, replacing the French Hotel. Across the street George Scribner built Scribner's Opera House, costing $20,000. Alphonse Weill used "his last dollar" to construct a fine new two-story brick building for his store. A new home for the Kern Valley Bank at the southwest corner of 18th and Chester was just being completed. The county voters also approved a huge bond issue of $250,000 to build an addition to the courthouse, to put up a much better jail and hospital, and to improve county roads.

Then Bakersfield residents held the greatest Fourth of July celebration ever in 1892. There was a wonderful parade with fireworks and picnics. For the people of Bakersfield, the long-awaited prosperity had finally come.

Pictured here is the Kern Guard, also known as the Bakersfield Militia. Garbed in a mix of Civil War uniforms, civilian clothes, and Prussian army surplus, the unit was formed in 1892 by J.M. Reuck.

The Rebuilders

BAKERSFIELD RISES FROM ASHES

It started in the Southern Hotel and was a real nice fire from a boy's point of view. The whole town went up in a glorious blaze. After that the town history dated from "before the fire" and "after the fire."
      —*Rush Maxwell Blodget*, Little Dramas of Old Bakersfield, *1931*

The big fire of July 7, 1889 changed the appearance of Bakersfield's business section more than anything until the 1952 earthquake. Eyewitnesses spotted the first smoke about nine o'clock on that hot Sunday morning in July. A great cloud of ash climbed lazily into the sky as the alarm went out. Everyone who was able quickly made his way toward the excitement. There were few church services held in Bakersfield that day.

Early arrivals found the Fish Building at 19th and Chester burning vigorously, and the nearby Southern Hotel, the finest hostelry in town, already on fire as was the Arlington House across the intersection. The fire fanned rapidly in all directions as a rising wind carried burning fragments from roof to roof. The clang of the fire bell could be heard as volunteer companies rolled into action, but there was little they could do. Most of the buildings were made of wood and underground conduits, designed to pump water for just such an emergency, were plugged with roots, leaving firefighters virtually helpless.

The fire spread both north and south on

This view from Scribner's water tower shows Bakersfield rebuilding after the 1889 fire. Courtesy, Kern County Museum

Chester Avenue, burning every building on the street from the slough, where 23rd Street is today, south to Truxtun Avenue. Buildings on both sides of 19th Street, east and west of Chester Avenue, were also destroyed. The flames leaped to several adjoining streets and blocks, and Bryant School, on the present side of the main fire station, was consumed. Only two buildings in the business district escaped the conflagration. One was St. Paul's Episcopal Church on the corner of 17th and Eye streets, thought by many to have been spared only by the hand of God. The other was the wooden Scribner water tower at 17th and Chester. A great effort had been made to preserve it so the town would not be without good water.

In three hours 15 city blocks were devastated. In all 147 businesses, 5 hotels, and 44 homes were gone and 1,500 people were homeless. There were no stores and no supplies. The three newspaper offices were ruined. But thanks to George Wear, the owner-editor of the *Gazette*, who had managed to save an old hand press and some cases of type, news of the big fire was published.

The once grand Southern Hotel stands in ruins after the 1889 fire that destroyed much of Bakersfield. Courtesy, Beale Memorial Library; Carlton Watkins Photo

The next morning wagonloads of meat, vegetables, and groceries came in from surrounding ranches. The drivers went house-to-house leaving whatever was needed free of charge. Haggin and Carr hauled in supplies from their company store on the Belleview Ranch and Sumner businessmen came forth with great generosity. Bales of clothing arrived for the stricken citizens as did money: Little Tehachapi sent $74.50 to help the unfortunate in Bakersfield. Offers of assistance also came from San Francisco, Los Angeles, Sacramento, and Fresno, but the people of Bakersfield were already busy rebuilding an even finer city.

A group of citizens met at the courthouse and courageously resolved "that from the ashes of our present affliction shall arise our future crown of glory." At first finances were a problem since little of the loss was covered by insurance and no bank in San Francisco would lend a cent toward Bakersfield's rebuilding program. Then Daniel Meyer and associates, San Francisco money lenders, graciously advanced the necessary cash.

Within two weeks 260 men were busy clearing lots, grading, excavating, and building. Enough temporary structures were put up to resume business, while permanent, more pretentious structures were erected out of brick. The main beneficiary of this sudden fondness for brick was James Curran and his Bakersfield Sandstone and Brick Company at the corner of Sonora and Eureka streets.

It was apparent as Bakersfield rebuilt that the townspeople hoped to create a more metro-politan appearance. Although the village in 1890 had a population of 3,563 persons, the city leaders anticipated 10,000 to 15,000 in five or six years. It was on this basis the new city rose from the ashes. Almost all the burned buildings were replaced by larger and finer ones.

The most remarkable new building was the Southern Hotel on the northwest corner of 19th and Chester, which was said to rival San Francisco's finest. It cost $110,000 to build, half of which came from the insurance paid on the burned hotel, and the rest from the pockets of Bakersfield businessmen who formed the Southern Hotel Association. Large enough for a city ten times the size of Bakersfield, the elegant building had three floors and 84 rooms all with hot and cold running water and gas. The bottom floor of the hotel was devoted to stores and offices, one of which housed the new Kern

This photo, taken from the water tower at 17th, looks north on Chester Avenue. Courtesy, Kern County Museum

County Land Company office.

Haggin and Tevis formed the Kern County Land Company in September 1890, soon after the big fire. They had invested at least four million dollars in their 14 Kern County ranches, and so far the financial return had not been very attractive. Encouraged by land and lot sales in 1888 and 1889, Haggin and Tevis formally organized their land holdings under the new company and drew up extensive plans for subdividing and colonizing.

Less than ecstatic about this development was Billy Carr, whose dream of making the Kern Delta the most beautiful and most productive spot in the world did not include the land being parceled and sold. When the

company replaced him by San Francisco real estate promoter S.W. Fergusson, Carr sold out to Haggin and Tevis. "Big Boss" Carr, the dynamic, manipulative genius of the Republican party, and of Union Pacific and Southern Pacific railroads, found he was no longer a force. On May 19, 1897, he was found accidentally asphyxiated in his hotel room in San Francisco.

The Kern County Land Company had gone ahead with its grand plan to develop four model colonies: Rosedale on 12,000 acres, Lerdo on 11,000, Union Avenue on 13,000, and Mountain View on 9,000. The land was divided into 20-acre farms that sold for $60 to $100 an acre, including water rights. Agricultural

The Kern County Land Company Building was located on 19th Street. Courtesy, Tenneco West

advice was included. The Kern County Land Company was anxious that all colonists be successful, and an experimental farm was set up in the Lerdo colony to test new crops and improve culture.

Throughout the U.S. and Europe an extensive publicity campaign told of "The Greatest Irrigated Farm in the World," with "climate nearly perfect," and soil "richer than the Nile Delta." The brochures suggested that with careful management it took very little time for the farms to be self-supporting and even profitable. People traveled from all over to inspect the model colonies and attend free promotional barbecues. Many of the would-be farmers were impressed and sales were reported to be brisk.

Many of the first settlers came from England,

where the company's promotion had been particularly strong. At Rosedale English farmers, who were accustomed to intensive farming on small acreages, were soon breaking the sod with a man behind a single plow pulled by a horse. This was a great joke to the workmen on the large ranches, where a large gang plow was pulled with 6 to 10 horses. But the steady Englishmen soon had grapes, peaches and plums, alfalfa and vegetables planted as recommended by the agricultural experts. By 1892 there were enough English colonists to build an Episcopal chapel at Rosedale called St. John's Episcopal Mission.

The new settlers soon found that successful farming required much more than just growing the crops. The high freight charges of the Southern Pacific had been a problem from the beginning. In 1893 the *Bakersfield Echo* commented, "Fresh peaches are bringing $1.00 for a twenty pound box in Chicago. The freight is 65 cents per box, leaving the shipper 35 cents." But the ingenious colonists built a small cannery to get their fruit to the market in more economical form. And the hardier and more practical hung on despite the national recession of 1893 and 1894.

A few of the English settlers were known as "remittance men" because they received a monthly check from their noble families in England. Bakersfield was glad to help them spend their money. One Bakersfield remittance man brought the town international fame. Lord Sholto Douglas, third son of the Marquis of Queensbury, wooed and won, with extensive journalistic attention, Miss Maggie Mooney, a showgirl from Tehachapi who performed on Frank Carson's stage on 20th Street.

Bakersfield, however, was making progress in its own right. The *History of the Counties of Fresno, Tulare, and Kern* of 1892 stated that within three years of the great fire, Bakersfield had "a truly metropolitan appearance . . . being lined with handsome buildings . . . and a large number of business houses carrying immense stocks." One of the most elaborate new homes built in the area was that of William Sanders Tevis, son of Lloyd Tevis. It was on the present-day site of the Stockdale Country Club. William had married Mabel Pacheco, daughter of Romualdo Pacheco, the governor of California in 1875. William, now a director for the Kern County Land Company, had grown up accustomed to great wealth and considered himself a capitalist like his father.

It was generally agreed that advances in Kern County education were due largely to

At the far right of this 1890s street scene is the Southern Hotel, located at 19th and Chester. Courtesy, Kern County Museum

The Kern Island Canal made possible the development of much county agriculture. Courtesy, Beale Memorial Library; Carlton Watkins Photo

This 1890s street scene looks east on 19th Street from the Post Office. Courtesy, Kern County Museum

county superintendent of schools Alfred Harrell. He was first elected in 1886 and had been returned to office ever since. He had organized the school system, established teaching standards, increased the school year to eight months, and raised teachers' salaries to $80 a month for men and $70 a month for women. His great ambition was to get Bakersfield an accredited high school so those desiring education would not have to leave the county. A bond issue was passed for $30,000, and construction on the new high school was begun. In the meantime high school classes began in the Railroad Avenue School on January 9, 1893, with 36 students. The next year "Kaycee High" continued in its own four-story building in the center of Elm Grove.

Although church attendance in Bakersfield was far behind saloon attendance, new churches were steadily added. The Baptist Church had been meeting in George Wear's Opera House since 1887 and later in the courthouse. In April 1890 the Baptists dedicated their own building, incorporating as the First Baptist Church of Bakersfield. Two years later the new additions were the First Congregational Church and the Mount Zion Baptist Church. The Chinese also built a new Joss House on the southwest corner of 18th and R streets.

But another rude awakening was in store for Bakersfield early in the morning on February 10, 1893. "Cowboys dashed from house to house to wake citizens with cries of 'Flood, flood, flee for your lives,'" according to Rush Blodget. Once again the Kern River had overflowed its banks, this time covering Chester Avenue with several feet of water and filling cellars with mud. Schoolboys let out of classes had a fine time poling rafts up and down the street, never worrying about the financial loss to the merchants, who were

The Tevis family residence in Stockdale is now the site of the Stockdale Country Club. Courtesy, Tenneco West

These three women were Kern County High School teachers in 1894. Pictured right to left are Ella Fay, Adaline Nicholson, and May Stark. Courtesy, Kern County Museum

already hard pressed by the depression of 1893.

That same year the little town of Sumner, where the Southern Pacific Railroad had chosen to place its depot, renamed itself Kern or Kern City. It had grown steadily and had voted to incorporate. The early business section encompassed four blocks. Stores and other establishments extended a block east and west of Baker, on Sumner facing the railroad track, and continued one block south of Sumner on Baker taking in both sides of the street.

Both the railroad depot and Bakersfield felt the effects of the "Great Railroad Strike," which closed down Kern County's railroads on June 28, 1894. Local trainmen struck in sympathy with railmen in Illinois. But for farmers who needed to send out early fruit, it

was very bad timing. Bakersfield had sufficient food and other necessities, but the town had to go without ice since it was brought in from Truckee by rail. Saloons were forced to sell warm beer to their customers, which didn't go over well in the middle of summer. The strike lasted until late in July, when it was broken by General William R. Shafter, who gained fame later in the Spanish American War.

By this time the Kern County Land Company officials decided they were tired of paying out money to promote the colonies. The directors fired S.W. Fergusson and made Henry A. Jastro general manager. Jastro had been associated with Haggin, Tevis, and Carr since 1874, the days of their first investments. He also had many interests of his own. Besides being

The first Kern County High School building was built in 1895. The site on which it stood is the current home of Bakersfield High School. Courtesy, Kern County Museum

In the great flood of 1893, the Kern River, swollen by melting snows and heavy rains, overran its banks to sweep through the downtown area. Courtesy, Ticor

chairman of the Kern County Board of Supervisors, he was director of two of Bakersfield's four banks, the Producers' Savings Bank and Bakersfield Building and Loan Association. Solomon Jewett ran the Kern Valley Bank and Simon W. Wible was president of the Bank of Bakersfield.

Jastro's challenge, as the new manager of the Kern County Land Company, was to bring money into the company rather than constantly spend it as his predecessors had done. He dropped all departments that weren't paying their way, which soon included most of the land salespeople. Property improvements were kept to a minimum unless the investment would directly improve income. Jastro did approve a company slaughterhouse and meat packing plant at the Bellevue ranch, which was completed in August 1897.

He encouraged other investments that he believed had good potential such as the Power Development Company's hydroelectric power plant, the first in Kern Canyon. Lloyd Tevis put up most of this money. A flume was built along the canyon wall to carry water from the intake

to a generator at the mouth of the canyon. A tunnel carved out of solid rock eventually replaced the flume. This provided electric power to Leonard P. St. Clair's Bakersfield Gas and Electric Light Company. St. Clair is credited as being the brain behind Bakersfield's pioneer electrical projects. Actually it was some time before the financial remuneration for the Power Development Company became interesting. Another Jastro project was the Electric Water Company. The Kern County Land Company bought the older Scribner Water Works and enlarged the water system to meet the needs of growing Bakersfield. These improvements added greatly to the whole area's potential for income and quality of life.

Another Bakersfield mover and shaker, school superintendent Alfred Harrell, purchased the *Bakersfield Californian* from George Weeks for $1,000. With a circulation of 300, the little four-page paper was published every Saturday. Harrell had no previous newspaper experience, but he became very interested and published his first editorial on January 26, 1897. He finished his school duties

the next year and then devoted all of his time to building up the best possible paper and in advancing Bakersfield and Kern County.

There was plenty to report the next year as growth picked up in Bakersfield. After the incorporation of Kern City, Bakersfield residents thought perhaps they should consider reincorporating their own town. Many were still opposed, but finally in a January 1898 vote, incorporation won 387 to 197. Bakersfield was incorporated as a city of the fifth class. Its city boundaries at that date were 34th Street on the north, 4th Street and Palm Street on the south, Union Avenue on the east, and Oak Street on the west.

May was a big month for the town. Early in the month about 85 of Kern County's young men were loaded on the Southern Pacific train for San Francisco. They made up Company G, Sixth Regiment, U.S. California Volunteer

Above middle: The Kern County Land Company was formed by James Huggin and Lloyd Tevis as the first large-scale development company in the area.

Opposite top: Pictured on 17th Street just south of Chester, Trolley No. 3 prepares for a last run before the conversion to electric trains. Courtesy, Kern County Museum

Opposite below: This tower held the 30,000-gallon tank of the Bakersfield Water Works. Water was pumped by steampower from the house at left. Courtesy, Beale Memorial Library; Carlton Watkins Photo

Infantry, which was called up during the Spanish American War. The month was also one of busy planning and great anticipation for the people of Bakersfield. The long-hoped-for "People's Railroad" had almost reached the town.

This new line was the result of the long suffering under the Southern Pacific monopoly over transportation between the San Joaquin Valley and San Francisco. When it was learned that Southern Pacific had made approximately $8 million or one fourth of their gross profit in 1894 in the San Joaquin Valley alone, a group of San Francisco businessmen decided there was room for a competing line. Of course there were no government land grants as earlier lines had received, but when a meeting was called, over $1 million was subscribed in 15 minutes. Stock was issued and people of every class bought shares, which earned it the name "People's Railroad."

George Weeks, then editor of the *Bakersfield Californian*, backed the Southern Pacific and scoffed at the new line until 50 prominent businessmen brought in a signed resolution in

Previous page, right: In the 1890s the Kern County Court House was rebuilt on this site at 16th and Chester.

These Chinese railroad workers lead a parade in celebration of the arrival of the San Francisco and San Joaquin Valley Railroad on May 27, 1898. The Southern Hotel at 19th and Chester is in the immediate background.

favor of the new road. In 1895 Weeks got out a special railroad edition of the newspaper, but it apparently was not enough to rescue his credibility. When Alfred Harrell purchased the paper, he was enthusiastic about the new road. He joined in on the great celebration plans set for May 27, 1898, when the first San Francisco and San Joaquin Valley Railroad train would arrive.

On the assigned day more than 1,000 people were at the station to greet the new train. At 10:30 a.m., the engine came into view, and let off a loud whistle, answered by bells

Randsburg in 1897 was a gold boomtown at the eastern edge of Kern County. The town today is little more than a wide spot in the road. Courtesy, Kern County Museum

and whistles all over Bakersfield. Decked out in flags and bunting, the engine pulled to a stop, unloading a full trainload of dignitaries and passengers who were greeted by happy Bakersfield and Kern County officials. They were ushered into carriages to join the "greatest procession in Bakersfield's history" down gaily decorated streets.

The parade ended at the brightly decorated Arlington House where speeches were interrupted with many cheers. After a sumptuous lunch and a tour to show the potential of the area, the crowd was treated to a balloon ascension from the county courthouse. In the evening a crowd gathered at the courthouse to enjoy a spectacular display of fireworks. It all ended with a Grand Ball in the new Kern County Land Company building.

After that notable, but exhausting day, everyone agreed with *Bakersfield Californian* editor Harrell who concluded that "Progress and prosperity unparalleled in its history is about to be entered upon by Bakersfield." But no one in the town guessed that the predicted prosperity would come from an entirely new industry.

The Boomers

RICHES, ROUGHNECKS, AND ROWDIES

In boom-town Bakersfield, saloons, dance halls, and sporting houses ran wide open. Men frantically leased and re-leased land, fighting with fists and sometimes with guns to maintain their claims. Claims were staked and jumped by the dozens, and if one group of promoters went broke another moved right in to take its place. Kern River had become a major California oil field.

—William Rintoul, Spudding In, *1976*

The Midway Sunset Fields in this photo give an impression of the impact of oil in Bakersfield. Courtesy, Getty Oil

True to predictions, competition from the new San Francisco & San Joaquin Valley line did produce results. The cost of both passenger tickets and freight began to fall immediately. Its service was friendly and courteous, and freight and passengers were delivered promptly. Investors, too, were pleased with their "handsome dividends."

After only about five months service, however, the startling headline appeared: "Santa Fe Owns the Valley Line." On October 20, 1898, the Santa Fe line bought the new railroad, at last realizing its goal of a line from Chicago to San Francisco. Everyone seemed pleased with the transaction: the owners and operators of the San Francisco & San Joaquin and the Santa Fe, as well as the customers. The new owners promised to retain all the employees and it was reported that they kept their word.

But even greater changes were in store for

Bakersfield after the 1899 discovery of oil on the Kern River. Tom Means was the owner of a small "ranch" seven miles northeast of Bakersfield, just east of present-day Gordon's Ferry. Believing in the existence of oil near the river, in the spring of 1899 Means induced James Elwood, a woodcutter, to dig for oil and gave him a lease on his property. Elwood and his father, Jonathan, enlisted the assistance of Milton McWorter who at the time was drilling in McKittrick, then called Asphalto.

Digging began under the bank almost level with the surface of the river. Using a simple auger-type drill, they cut a three-inch hole. After several failures they struck oil sand at 13 feet. The Elwoods then excavated a shaft on top of the bank above. Laboriously digging with pick and shovel, they struck the same oil sand at 43 feet. They screwed an auger bit on the end of several lengths of pipe. By hand turning a wooden crosspiece clamped to the top section,

Tom Means provided the impetus and the land for the first oil well in Bakersfield. The well had a profound impact on Bakersfield's economic future. Courtesy, Kern County Museum

they drilled another 30 feet. Soon about two barrels of oil rose daily. Nineteen days later, the first drilled well on the Kern River was completed, on July 26, 1899. This well continued to flow for quite a few years, although it was never a big producer.

At first no one believed this oil came from along the Kern River. Some folks suggested the well had been "salted" with McKittrick oil, which it closely resembled. But the doubters finally were satisfied when Edward L. Doheny, the famous oil man from Los Angeles, bought out Tom Means.

As the word spread people flocked in to see the new oil well. All kinds of people staked claims and defended them. Dry holes were few. Clusters of tents and shacks quickly appeared in the hills and on the riverbank near the first well. This was the beginning of Oil Center, which at one time had a population of 5,000. By 1901 the nearby Oil City would be the greatest shipping point for petroleum in California.

Not surprisingly Bakersfield and Kern (formerly Sumner) boomed. People and money flowed in at an accelerating rate in the early years of the century to build communities with more beautiful homes and more impressive

public and business buildings. And for Bakersfield there were other improvements.

The old horse-drawn trolley cars were replaced by the Bakersfield and Kern Electric Railway in 1901. The power came from the Power, Transit, and Light Company's electric plant at the mouth of Kern Canyon. Several important buildings were added downtown, including the handsome new Masonic Temple at the corner of Chester Avenue and 20th, and theaters and halls were added liberally.

At the dawn of 1902 the Kern River Oil Field

A turn-of-the-century oil derrick stands in this photo as a representation of the beginnings of the Kern Oil Empire. This industry "has meant more to the state than its great movie, citrus, fishing and tourist incomes combined," according to the California State Chamber of Commerce. Courtesy, Kern County Museum

broke all previous production records, encouraging oil development on the west side of the valley as well. The Sunset Railroad was a joint venture of the Southern Pacific and Santa Fe to connect Bakersfield with the Sunset Oil Field in the southwest San Joaquin.

The success of the new industry and influx of workers also encouraged Bakersfield's first Labor Day celebration on September 3, 1902. The Kern County Council of Labor had been chartered by the American Federation of Labor the year before. The council included many now-defunct unions: the Amalgamated Street Railways Employees' Union, the Blacksmith's Union, the Brewers Union, and the Cigar Makers Union.

An unpleasant side effect came with the oil boom as Bakersfield became known as the worst in the West for prostitution, gambling, drunkenness, and vice. A tenderloin district had developed, where violent death was almost commonplace. Bounded by M Street on the east, L Street on the west, 19th Street on the south, and 22nd Street on the north, laughter rang day and night from large dance halls, saloons, and gambling halls. Painted ladies gestured from their cribs to men sauntering by. The "cribs" were single rooms with one bed used for prostitution. The Chinese had settled in this area in the early days, but the proprietors of most of these establishments were not Oriental.

On April 19, 1903, a bright Sunday morning, while the other side of town got ready for church, shots suddenly rang out from the tenderloin. This was no ordinary shooting. The "toughest outlaw of the West," James McKinney, had been blasted by the shotgun of Burt Tibbet in a shoot-out at the Chinese Joss House on L Street. But before he went down McKinney had killed Deputy Marshal Will Tibbet and fatally injured City Marshal Jeff Packard who died the next morning. Although McKinney's death in Bakersfield marked "the end of the western badman as an authentic figure in American history," as historian Joe Doctor put it, the people of Bakersfield were not pleased that this seamy incident got so much publicity.

One of the first electric trolley cars which replaced the horse-drawn cars is pictured here. Courtesy, Kern County Museum

Fortunately, good publicity was coming from other sectors. The city received a handsome gift from Truxtun Beale that would be recognized as its trademark. The 64-foot clock tower of Moorish design was dedicated April 2, 1904, as a memorial to Beale's mother. It was patterned after a tower Beale had seen in Spain during his term as United States Ambassador there. The city trustees put it at the intersection of 17th and Chester. As a gesture of gratitude, the city renamed Railroad Avenue, Truxtun, in his honor.

The news from the Kern River Oil Field was not doing the town any harm either. In 1904 it produced more oil than any other field in California, with 17.5 million barrels. But the glut caused the price of oil to bottom out from its peak at a dollar a barrel to 11 cents. Many small companies failed. Nineteen other companies managed to survive by banding together on November 3, 1904, as the Independent Oil Producers Agency. The agency marketed the oil at the best price possible.

Despite the falling price of oil, by 1907

Bakersfield was bursting with a population of 7,338. New people were coming in each day and to meet their needs, Edison's Kern River No. 1, the largest hydroelectric plant in the United States, began generating power on May 19, 1907. In addition, the city was constructing a sewer system capable of serving 20,000 people.

By the next year Bakersfield was the acknowledged center of California's oil industry. Money, workers, and equipment for both the Kern River and West Side oil fields radiated from Bakersfield. A weekly magazine, written and published in Bakersfield, *California Oil World,* also began in 1908. New uses were developing for petroleum, and the price of oil was headed back up. New businesses were forming, there were now 150 member companies in the Independent Oil Producers Agency, and every company was pioneering in methods of locating, drilling, and extracting oil.

What this all meant for Bakersfield was yet more growth. In the year 1909 alone a record amount of building cost more than $220,000 and 53 buildings were still under construction. Chester Avenue became a "theater row," a new hospital was started by the Sisters of Mercy, and beautiful new churches dotted the city.

The new churches added a bolder voice against Bakersfield's vice, drunkenness, and thievery, as the tenderloin district was still one of the roughest in the West. Anti-gambling and anti-saloon citizen organizations were formed asking for stricter regulations and better

George Helm (left), owner of the Crawford Bar, stands in his establishment in this 1911 photo. Courtesy, Kern County Museum

enforcement. An undersheriff, constable, and 30 citizens raided the Palace, Standard, and Owl dance halls and arrested their keepers; but when brought to trial, the justice of the peace acquitted them. In a citizens' crusade sweep, the arrested gamblers pleaded guilty, and the craps and roulette tables were shipped off to Nevada.

The town got another big boost when, after several elections, the people of Bakersfield and Kern agreed to consolidate. After that Kern City was known as East Bakersfield. The first consolidated city election was held July 1910. One of the first results of the consolidation was the paving of 19th Street, connecting the two business centers in 1910. The city bought street-building equipment, and within two years streets along 200 blocks had been paved at a cost of half a million dollars.

The new roads were especially appreciated by the few people who had automobiles. By 1910 there were at least 200 cars in Kern County. Automobile owners also had the option of braving the terrible roads in surrounding areas to see how the countryside was developing. Even land far from the Kern River was changing from prairie to irrigated farmland. The new farms were the result of better wells, better pumps, and cheaper gasoline. Pump irrigated farming was successful around Delano and at Rio Bravo, and also on Kern County Land Company land in Rosedale and Stockdale. Fledgling communities at Wasco, McFarland, Arvin, and Buttonwillow also got their starts in this boom era.

Actually improvements in county roads were not long in coming. On July 8, 1913, a bond issue of $2.5 million was passed to improve county roads. Graded and paved roads were made as quickly as possible from Bakersfield to the West Side oil centers of Taft, Maricopa, and McKittrick, and these towns to each other. Wasco finally had a good paved highway to Lost Hills, Rio Bravo, and McFarland. Delano got a good road to the Tulare County line. The Sand Cut and the Weedpatch loop ran into Bakersfield, paved all the way.

These roads, however, were not ready in December 1909, when carloads of armed men left Bakersfield for the West Side oil fields of Midway, Elk Hills, and Buena Vista Hills. These men were determined to take and hold as much

as they could of the rich oil land. By New Year's morning, the hills of these oil fields were dotted with white claim notices. Beside each notice stood armed guards.

This was the beginning of Kern County's second and biggest oil boom. The price of oil had come back up and the market had expanded. This naturally stimulated oil exploration. In 1909 rich flowing oil wells in the Midway Field and great gas wells in the Buena Vista Hills were brought into production on land that had recently been taken from public domain under placer mining laws.

When word of this activity got back to Washington, the fear that all oil-rich lands would pass out of federal ownership prompted President William Taft to withdraw from sale all San Joaquin Valley land that could be oil bearing. But little attention was paid to this order because oil men believed it exceeded the President's power. Instead the order stimulated locators to hurry up and file additional oil claims. In 1910 Congress passed legislation

backing up Taft's withdrawal, and he reissued his order on July 2, 1910. This left in question the legality of the claims between the two orders. Representative Sylvester C. Smith of Bakersfield, however, succeeded in getting a bill through Congress to strengthen the claims between the two executive withdrawal orders.

This created a second boom, which packed hotels in Bakersfield, McKittrick, and Maricopa. Taft (formerly Moro and later Moron) sprang to life, then burned and was rebuilt again with lots at fantastic prices. The rush was so great that all the lumber in Kern County was quickly used up. Every available train and wagon was used to bring in oil field equipment and timber for derricks. For nearly a year the Sunset Railroad between Bakersfield and Taft was the most profitable line in the world.

Kern County itself became world famous for its oil gushers, the most spectacular of which for months put out 68,000 barrels a day. It spewed a stream of oil 20 feet wide and 200 feet high, drenching everything for miles around.

The Kern County Court House served Kern County from 1912 until 1952 when it was demolished because of damage it suffered in the earthquake. The site that this building occupied is the same site as the present courts and administration building.

Opposite: The Beale Memorial Clocktower was built in 1904 by Truxtun Beale as a memorial to his mother. During his term as the ambassador to Spain he was inspired by a clock-tower there. The tower stood as a landmark for the people of Bakersfield until the 1952 earthquake. It was reconstructed in 1964 at its current site on the grounds of the Kern County Museum.

Derrick Avenue in Sunset Fields is a typical oil field scene.

Modest beginnings gave way to Bakersfield's emergence as an "oil town." Courtesy, Kern County Museum

No one had any idea how to cap it. Spectators came by car and train to see the dramatic spectacle. Suddenly, after over a year of spouting, the gusher stopped. But not before 10 million barrels of oil had been vomited up, with only about half of it saved. There was more trouble because the Lakeview No. 1 and other gushers produced far more oil than the market could absorb and brought the price of oil to a new low.

The next few years were busy ones for the people of Bakersfield. The Buena Vista Hills now were sending a steady supply of natural gas to Los Angeles by pipeline. San Joaquin Light and Power Company, a forerunner of the Pacific Gas and Electric Company, bought Bakersfield Electric Company, including the streetcar line. The second oil boom created another construction boom. The new three-story San Joaquin Hospital was built in 1910, the next year a new courthouse was built on two blocks between 15th and 17th streets on Chester, and in 1913 the county began a jail on the north of Truxton between P and Q streets. Bakersfield also gained the distinction in 1913 of forming the oldest continuously running junior college in California. Thirteen students attended Bakersfield Junior College the first year in the basement of the high school. It was about this time that the Kern Fair Association

The Lakeview No. 1 gusher, reflected in a pool of oil, was a most spectacular sight. People came by excursion train from all parts of the state to view it. Much oil was lost but about five million barrels were saved by earthen dams created to form large oil reservoirs.

The San Joaquin Light and Power Corporation used this horse-drawn wagon to carry its first crew for meter installations. Courtesy, Ticor

was organized. The land that the Kern County Museum still occupies was bought for fairgrounds, and a splendid racetrack was designed and constructed.

Everyone in Bakersfield and Kern County benefited when a shorter and better road was put through to Los Angeles. Officials of the State Highway Commission decided to lay the road straight across the mountains north of Castaic and over La Liebre Range, a route 60 miles shorter than the most popular existing road.

A huge road-building project even for the state to undertake, it was dubbed the Ridge Route Road, and was noted for its circuitous switchbacks and steep ascents and descents. After a year of work, the new, unpaved road was opened in October 1915. As primitive as it was, the road quickly became popular, and motor stage lines soon switched over to this improved and shorter route. This road became an important artery connecting Bakersfield and the southern San Joaquin to southern California.

When the United States entered World War I

on April 6, 1917, everybody in the now-prosperous city sprang into patriotic action. Twenty thousand people watched 7,000 marchers in a patriotic demonstration on April 13 that included 23 veterans of the Civil War and 60 members of Herman's Sons, a German lodge whose members were eager to display their loyalty to the United States. Altogether Kern County sent 3,676 men off to fight. Of this number 100 would never return.

At home agricultural production went into high gear. The next summer's crop production was boosted 300 percent. Oil production also went up with income totaling $4.5 million per month. Residents were so enthusiastic about buying Liberty Bonds that a United States merchant ship was named "Bakersfield." And Kern County was the only California county to send twice as much money as the Red Cross asked for in its Christmas drive.

When at last the Armistice was signed and the men began returning home, the Frank S. Reynolds Post Number 26 of the American Legion helped many Bakersfield veterans re-adjust to civilian life. Organized in the spring of

This 1930s photo shows Highway 99, the tortuous route commonly referred to as "The Grapevine." Although it is now eight lanes of Interstate 5, the steep grade is not much easier to negotiate.

1919, the post was named for a Bakersfield man who had died in action. Among its many functions, the post put out the first legion newspaper, *American Legion Weekly*, which served as a model for the state and national papers, and maintained an employment service for veterans. When construction of the legion hall was started in January 1923, Herbert Hoover turned the first shovelful (before anyone anticipated he would become President in 1929).

Another postwar organization with less benevolent intentions was the Ku Klux Klan. Sheriff LeRoy Galyen remembered hundreds of white-robed and hooded klansmen holding ceremonies around burning crosses. So many people were beaten, robbed, and threatened

that the Kern County Grand Jury was asked to investigate. The board of supervisors and the city council were asked to make wearing a disguise a misdemeanor, which they did.

A sheriff's raid of the office of the local "Grand Goblin" elicited a list of all Kern County members, which was published in the *Bakersfield Californian*. The names of a number of county supervisors and city council members appeared on the list, and all but one was recalled. District attorney Jesse Dorsey zealously prosecuted Klan members for criminal actions. By 1924 it was reported the Klan had disbanded in Kern County, which may or may not have been true.

There were other readjustments after the war. There was the problem of cutting

This San Joaquin Light and Power Company crew was a precursor of today's Pacific Gas and Electric Company. Courtesy, Ticor

The Grand Hotel resulted from the construction boom that came with the inflow of money after the discovery of oil. Courtesy, Kern County Museum

The intersection of 19th and Chester has long been the center of downtown Bakersfield. Courtesy, Kern County Museum

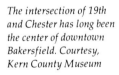

production from wartime levels, as well as reemploying veterans. Demand and prices on everything were going down, while the numbers needing jobs had increased. Unions, of course, attempted to protect their members. The result was a series of strikes, starting with telephone operators in 1919 and a nationwide railway wage dispute that tied up all Santa Fe service for a week in August of 1922.

But the strike that had the most effect on Bakersfield and the West Side came when oil workers walked out in 1921. The price of oil

had fallen by a third, and producers announced that pay would be cut by a dollar a day. The workers asked for a guarantee of no further cuts for a year; but since the oil market was so unstable, the producers felt they could not sign such a promise. So on September 11, 8,000 men walked off the job.

The union organized "law and order patrols" to guard against strikebreakers. They stopped all cars entering the oil fields, and if a driver refused to stop, the "law and order patrol" was apt to shoot. Since many of the roads were used by regular traffic, this caused considerable objection. The situation was finally resolved when the United States Secretary of Labor asked the district union to call the strike off. A total of 7,000 workers reported back to work, but the oil producers were unable to use them all and many remained unemployed. This strike seriously retarded business in Bakersfield and the West Side towns, and left many men without paychecks and some families without homes.

New employment opportunities were developing, however, many of which were attributable to the much increased use of the automobile. Paving of the Ridge Route began right after the war. The state supervised the work, hiring day laborers to save money, but it was still close to a $1 million project. The two-

lane, 20-foot wide roadbed was covered with four and a half inches of reinforced concrete. By 1920 the entire route from Bakersfield into Los Angeles was complete.

In Bakersfield, too, the now-commonplace automobile was causing changes. Chester Avenue had become "automobile row" because of the new brick buildings for auto agencies. Livery stables and other businesses changed over to accommodate cars, either selling or learning to service them.

Another sign of change came when Kern County elected a woman to the State Assembly. Grace Dorris won office in 1919 just before women earned the right to vote in 1920. She introduced a resolution commemorating Congress when it passed the woman's suffrage amendment, and she was elected to another two-year term in 1923.

Another important development in Bakersfield and the surrounding communities in the "Roaring Twenties" came in part due to the work of the Cotton Experiment Station at Shafter. Careful experiments done on cotton culture at the station under William B. Camp and other outstanding agronomists made "white gold" an important addition to Kern County income. In the 1920s cotton became the most valuable agricultural crop in the southern valley and Kern County quickly became the

largest one-variety cotton region in the world. Additional income came from grapes, white potatoes, melons, and citrus fruits. Alfalfa, a standby since Colonel Baker's time, continued as an important staple and dairies steadily improved their products.

The result in Bakersfield during the decade was the outlay of several million dollars for new business buildings in the center of town. Among them was the new home of the *Bakersfield Californian* on the corner of 17th and I streets in 1926. In 1928 Alfred Harrell purchased the *Bakersfield Morning Echo*, his longtime rival. There was no doubt that Harrell's *Californian* would continue to dominate.

New elaborate movie theaters were added in

Top: Mrs. Fannie Tracy of Buttonwillow began raising ostriches just after the turn of the century. She became known as the "Buttonwillow Bird Lady" for the plumes she sold to the ladies' fashion industry. Courtesy, Kern County Museum

Above: The Rio Bravo Cotton Gin was on land that boasted one of the highest yields per acre of cotton. Courtesy, Kern County Museum

Kern County has long been an important producer of cotton. Pickers weigh their harvest in this 1920s photo.

Thinning cotton in the early 1900s was done much the same way as it is today. Courtesy, Kern County Museum

the twenties. The theaters seldom made artistic live presentations any more. But the Bakersfield Musical Association, organized in 1920, brought artists of national and international fame to packed audiences. Singers such as Lawrence Tibbet of the Metropolitan Opera (the son of Will Tibbet, the marshal killed in the shoot-out with gunman Jim McKinney in Bakersfield in 1903) were always received with great enthusiasm.

Sports continued to play an important role in Bakersfield's leisure-time pursuits. Most popular were Kern County Union High football games. In 1908, 1909, and 1917 the team won the San Joaquin Valley championship. But in 1916, 1920, 1921, 1922, 1923, and again in 1927, it won the state championship. The whole town turned out for these events.

In 1927 the board of supervisors purchased 160 acres north of Oildale for an airport site. The complete complex was said to be the finest county-owned airport on the Pacific Coast. It was named Meadows Field in honor of Cecil Meadows, aviation pioneer and airport superintendent for many years.

In 1928 the Kern County Chamber of Commerce, actually the reorganized Kern County Board of Trade, remained very active in working for the city's development. The board of supervisors built a special building for the Chamber in 1928 on Golden State Highway, the main route through the city. With the supervisors firmly behind them, by the next year the chamber had plenty to promote.

By 1929 Bakersfield boasted 34,000 citizens within its city limits and 60,000 within the surrounding area. The population had doubled during the decade. New homes lined much of Bakersfield's 12,553 miles of streets stretching across now nearly 4,470 acres. Seventy million dollars worth of business went through its five banks each year. There were 12 hotels, 2 golf and country clubs, 15 elementary schools, one junior high school and one of the finest high school-junior colleges in the country, 15 churches, and 60 social and service clubs. The city had an air of pride and permanence. There was no doubt that Bakersfield was now the "Queen of the South San Joaquin," just as Colonel Baker had prophesied only 70 years earlier.

An early lineup of planes at the Kern County Airport includes, at left, a Ryan M-1. The M-1's were the United States' first production monoplanes and the same plane Charles Lindberg flew on his historic transatlantic flight. Courtesy, Kern County Museum

The Survivors

A MODERN CITY EMERGES

By Howie Wines and Gene Hanson

The people who made this city were those who planned, worked, and directed the production of better homes, farms, industries, organizations, and people.

—*Jesse D. Stockton,* Those Who Serve, *1944*

The outlook for Bakersfield changed radically when the stock market crashed in 1929. Buffered at first by the diversity of its economic base, Bakersfield felt the effects of the Great Depression gradually. But as the Depression deepened, automobile sales slumped sharply and local merchants observed a marked decline in business. New construction dropped to an unprecedented low and the *Bakersfield Californian* was filled with tales of business failures. Local relief agencies were hard pressed to help the city's own residents, not to mention newcomers drifting in to seek employment. Farmers were particularly hard hit. With hogs at two cents a pound and cattle at three or four cents, these groups relied heavily on trading crops and livestock for necessities. Bakersfield banks, however, weathered the worst part of the Depression better than their counterparts in many areas of the nation. Not one bank in the city went under.

Things began to look better in the city after the election of President Franklin D. Roosevelt. Campaigning in California in 1932, Roosevelt had promised "not a mere change of party, but

a change of principles—a new deal." From 1933 to 1939 New Deal agencies poured millions of dollars into Bakersfield, which put thousands of people to work. The Public Works Administration (PWA) and the Works Progress Administration (WPA), through public agencies, financed scores of bridges, culverts, public buildings, overpasses, parks, and hundreds of miles of roads. Organized labor, churches, and service clubs were also very supportive of the New Deal, and thousands of volunteers did their share to help the less fortunate.

The economic hard times made people more eager than ever to escape the grim reality of everyday life. Kindled perhaps by the desire to remember happier times, in 1931 a few old-timers founded the Kern County Historical Society with teacher-turned-newspaperman Alfred Harrell as president. Bakersfield residents flocked to theaters and dance halls, which prospered during the 1930s. Hollywood responded to this cry for escapism by producing lavish musicals and lighthearted movies. With the repeal of Prohibition in 1933,

This 1930s photo looking south on Baker Street from Kentucky captures the growing city not far removed from frontier days.

This 1930 photo shows the Fiat truck that Richfield used to make the first bulk gasoline deliveries in Kern County. Courtesy, Ticor

many saloons reopened and prostitution revived. Church and relief groups complained that some working men were spending family food money on things other than food and family.

While Bakersfield struggled to free itself from the Depression, the international situation was deteriorating. War broke out in Europe in 1939; but Bakersfield residents were stunned when on Sunday morning, December 7, 1941, they heard on the radio that Japanese planes were bombing Pearl Harbor. The following day, 66 men crowded into Bakersfield recruiting offices. By December 9 there were so many volunteers that nobody kept count of them. The State Guard, commanded by Captain Leonard Hall, met at the fairgrounds; and in January 1942 the unit was expanded to six officers and 180 enlisted men. The pay was only two dollars a day for the two platoons of men who volunteered for active duty.

Just about everybody in Bakersfield pitched into the fight in some way. In all of the war loan drives, the town exceeded its quotas and

goals. Residents also filled buckets of sand to fight incendiary bombs and practiced blackout procedures. Boy Scouts and other youth groups collected and turned in scrap metal, newspapers, and tin cans. The "kitchen commandoes" saved grease (used for munitions) that was taken to local butcher shops and redeemed for ration stamps, which were needed to buy sugar, meat, coffee, dairy products, rubber, and cigarettes.

Because of its oil production facilities, Bakersfield had been tagged by the military as one of the state's major areas to be defended. In response Kern County and Bakersfield each formed parallel defense councils. The Kern County Defense Council and its Bakersfield counterpart developed air raid warning programs and communications systems. Both councils concentrated on improving protective services and coordinated operations of the fire and police departments, rescue and bomb squads, emergency food and housing crews, medical facilities, and utilities and public works divisions.

Defense and war-related industries provided hundreds of jobs for Bakersfield residents during the war. Many worked at Minter Field, which was a basic pilot training center until April 14, 1945. Records indicate that 11,265 Army Air Corps Cadets were graduated, some of whom became senior members of Britain's Royal Air Force. The Civil Air Patrol was established in February 1942, and Kern County Airport Superintendent Cecil Meadows announced that some 250 civilian pilots had the opportunity to join. Further wartime employment opportunities came with Lockheed Aircraft Component Factories and Vega Aircraft Company, a small plant producing ammunition boxes, and a dehydrating plant producing the infamous "K Rations."

Another now-infamous aspect of this era was the wave of public sentiment against aliens from the three Axis countries. By February 12, 1941, 411 alien Japanese had been confined on DiGiorgio land in Delano and Arvin. German aliens were interned near Shafter and there was reportedly a camp near Lamont. All Americans of Japanese, German, and Italian descent were restricted to their homes between 8 p.m. and 6 a.m. and were permitted to travel no more than five miles unless enroute to or from their places of business. All had to forfeit radios, cameras, explosives, and firearms.

But this travesty was overshadowed at the time by the county's fixation with the 14,000 Kern men who were under arms. In all 462 Kern County families may have questioned the cost of victory. The first to die had been Lt. William G. Sylvester, who fell at Hickam Field, on the island of Oahu, on the day Pearl Harbor

was attacked. Lieutenant Sylvester's brother, Robert, was later killed in action on July 3, 1943.

When it was over, the pent-up emotions of three years and eight months of war were released when Bakersfield's 75,000 residents poured into the streets in a celebration that lasted for hours. The first official flash of peace was noted by air raid sirens, church bells, and automobile horns at 4 p.m., Tuesday,

Predecessor to the Bakersfield Inn, the Motel Bakersfield coined the word for motor-hotel in the 1920s. With the growth of car and truck traffic, Bakersfield, on California's major north-south traffic route, was in an ideal location for just such an enterprise. Courtesy, Ticor

This 1931 photo shows the Union Avenue crossing of the Southern Pacific tracks. Courtesy, Kern County Museum

August 14, 1945. The celebrations were boisterous with spontaneous parades forming, and the air filling with confetti as celebrants atop the city's highest buildings tore up papers and telephone books.

Bars and package liquor stores were closed immediately. The sheriff and police departments were prepared for violence in the victory observance and officers turned out ready to devote the night to keeping over-zealous celebrants in line, but there was no drunken fighting in Bakersfield. Celebrants made the front of the American Legion hall a site for a wild, happy street dance. Complete strangers became friends on every street corner.

Churches all over town were filled with joyful parishioners united in prayers of thanksgiving. And although the long-awaited taste of victory was satisfying for the people of Bakersfield and Kern County, the biggest battle still lay ahead.

For more than a century Bakersfield residents had battled floods, fires, and earthquakes. But the earthquake of August 22, 1952, was, without doubt, Bakersfield's greatest catastrophe from a structural and financial viewpoint. The business, educational, religious, and social face of the city changed almost beyond recognition.

About a month earlier, on July 21, a terrifying series of earthquakes shook the Sierra

The earthquake of 1952 changed the face of Bakersfield more than any other event since the fire of 1889. City and county buildings, churches, hospitals, and various landmarks were damaged or destroyed and the city underwent total reconstruction. Courtesy, Kern County Museum

A reminder of the force of seismic upheaval, these railroad tracks were thrown 22 feet off center by the 1952 earthquake. Courtesy, Kern County Museum

Nevada and the valley floor. Much of Tehachapi and Arvin was destroyed, but Bakersfield rode out the quakes, suffering little damage. These tremblors disrupted irrigation systems for miles around, slopped water out of canals, caused reservoir walls to slump, toppled water tanks from their towers, and shifted farmhouses from their foundations. Rows of cotton were offset as much as 40 inches and railway tunnels twisted in on themselves. The nearby Paloma Refinery burst into flames, and transformers around Bakersfield exploded in blue-white spurts of fire. All four faces of the Beale Memorial Clock Tower fell, and were shattered on the pavement below.

But the Tehachapi earthquake, which registered at 7.5 on the Richter Scale, was only the beginning. Between July 21 and August 22 seismographs recorded 7 shocks at magnitudes of 6.0 or higher, 24 shocks at more than 5.0 on the scales, and 180 higher than 4.0. Everybody stopped counting the number of shocks below 4.0 after they had exceeded 300 in number.

It may have been this series of smaller earthquakes, however, that kept loss of life in

the "big" earthquake so low. On Friday, August 22, many buildings had already been evacuated, others had been strengthened by steel hoops or protected by scaffolding. Fire walls had been pulled down from structures, and dangerous ornamental facings had been removed. Meanwhile residents had learned what to do during and after a tremblor and when it finally hit, a surprising number of people stood under solid doorways or dived beneath desks instead of running into the streets.

"The Bakersfield earthquake, according to the United States Coast and Geodetic Survey, released energy equivalent to 2,000 atomic bombs," wrote Darrell Berrigan in the *Saturday Evening Post*. The earth, obeying the upward thrust of the Sierra Nevada and the downward pull of the alluvial valleys, had shifted about three feet along what is known as the White Wolf Fault.

Jim Day, editor of the *Bakersfield Californian*, was standing on the corner of 19th and Chester streets when the earthquake hit. He looked at

A 1938 photo of the intersection of 19th and Chester shows the one-time landmark Southern Hotel on the northwest corner. Courtesy, Kern County Museum

This 1946 photo shows the service community that arose at the summit of the Grapevine. Courtesy, Ticor

his watch, which read 3:42 on the hot August afternoon. The entire city, with a deep-throated, cracking roar, rose in the air, dropped, shuddered, and rose again. Thousands of tons of bricks thundered into the streets. Plate glass windows smashed, scattering jagged fragments of glass on the sidewalks. A mighty cloud of dust rose high over the city, blurring the sun, and darkening the streets—followed by silence. In only 25 seconds, less than half a minute, the city had been transformed.

Muffled screams came from Lerner's Dress Shop, on 19th, where the fire wall from an adjoining building had crashed through the roof. Men ran from places of safety to help the trapped women. Mrs. Edna Ledbetter, a 25-year-old McFarland housewife, was found dead. Further east on 19th, a part of the two-story Kern County Equipment Company building collapsed. Pat Cozby, a 67-year-old clerk, died there. But amazingly, these were the only two fatalities. In all 32 people were injured, 8 of them seriously.

Chief of Police Horace V. Grayson and Fire

At the time of the earthquake in 1952, Earl Warren was still governor of California. Here the soon-to-be Chief Justice is pictured inspecting the damage his hometown suffered. Courtesy, Ticor

Chief Phil C. Pifer attributed the small loss of life to the fact that the earthquake lasted only a few seconds, and thus people had no time to run from buildings into the shower of falling masonry. Probably even more important was the fact that there was no aftershock, as is usual, to complete the destruction of buildings.

California Governor Earl Warren telephoned within a few minutes of the jolt with offers of help, but the people of Bakersfield turned them down. "We can handle the situation ourselves and grow forward," was their reply. There was no panic at any time. Not a single case of looting was reported and only one fire broke out, the result of a pilot light on a hot water heater igniting a leak in a gas pipe. According to the chamber of commerce, not a single Bakersfield business was forced to close, except temporarily for repairs.

The earthquake would have shaken a town with less spirit right off of the map. But for Bakersfield, rebuilding was a catalyst that began an economic chain reaction that continues to mushroom.

The 1950s brought on many of the changes that still characterize the modern city. Bakersfield entered the television age with

Bakersfield in 1948 was expanding with the beginning of the post-World War II population shift to the West. This aerial photo shows the clear demarcation between the city on the floodplain and the foothills. Courtesy, Kern County Museum

KBAK-TV, which was followed by KERO-TV. The Chinese Ying Ming Hall was dedicated in 1953, and, in that same year, Kern County boasted the world's deepest oil well. It was the Paloma well, drilled to a depth of 20,521 feet by the Ohio Oil Company. Another addition was the Isabella Dam, erected after five years of construction at a cost of $21 million. In 1954 Bakersfield gained yet another industry when a uranium boom changed many lives in the city. The busy Meadows Field gained a new Air Terminal Building in 1958. And the following year KGET was on the air, giving the town its

third television channel.

Perhaps inspired by the radical alterations to Bakersfield during the 1950s, residents voted to take a larger role in selecting their city leaders. Ever since its original incorporation, Bakersfield's mayor had been selected from the ranks of the city council. But in 1956 the people decided to separate the two offices and voted to establish a part-time mayor. In January 1957 Frank Sullivan, who had served on the city council since 1951, became the city's first elected mayor.

Four years later as a new decade dawned in

A 1966 aerial view of Bakersfield shows a modern city that did not suffer lasting aftereffects from the 1952 earthquake. Courtesy, Ticor

Bakersfield, Gene Winer, owner of an auto agency, succeeded Sullivan as mayor. The residents of Bakersfield in 1960 numbered about 59,000 and that year the Bakersfield Chamber of Commerce publication, *Metro,* stated that progress was steady: "Metropolitan Bakersfield's industrial growth in the past 12 months will result in the hiring of 238 persons [and] an increased payroll of $1,190,000." Overall capital investment stood at $2.4 million.

Tourism further boosted the city's economy in the early 1960s when ground was broken for California's newest and finest civic auditorium.

This was the result of some intense lobbying by a group of future-minded citizens and city leaders who forwarded their belief that Bakersfield needed to attract more conventions. After several years of planning, arguing, and scratching for funds, construction began in 1960. On November 11, 1962, at a cost of $5.5 million, the Bakersfield Civic Auditorium was dedicated. The first event open to the public on November 20, 1962, featured the world famous Ice Capades. Since then the Civic Auditorium has presented virtually all segments of the entertainment industry, bringing millions into the local economy.

A number of other construction projects marked Mayor Winer's four years. Two new highways were completed: Highway 99, which bypassed Bakersfield, and the Crosstown Freeway (178). A new high school, Foothill, sprang up, and the historic Beale Memorial Clock Tower, damaged by the earthquake, was restored and placed in the Kern County Museum. Gene Winer also arranged for an international sibling for Bakersfield: sister-city Wakayama, Japan.

From a vastly different background, Bakersfield's next city leader, elected in 1964, was Russell V. Karlen, a medical doctor who specialized in radiology. Dr. Karlen actively sought the 1964 World's Fair for Bakersfield, now a town of about 62,000, meeting with

99

officials and offering a site west of Highway 99 near California Avenue. He felt that if Bakersfield could host the World's Fair, the site could be used later as a four-year state college. The state college would come, but the California State College ("Cal State,") chartered in 1965 with first classes held in 1970, came a bit further to the west on Stockdale Highway. During his term Mayor Karlen and his family visited sister-city Wakayama, Japan, on behalf of the people of Bakersfield; the people themselves did the celebrating on behalf of Kern County's Centennial in 1966.

Rounding out the decade of the sixties as mayor was native son and civic leader, Don Hart, an auto dealer by trade. Serving 12 years in three consecutive terms, Hart was an influential force in Bakersfield throughout the 1970s. Although the population of Bakersfield boomed during his administration by 50 percent, from 69,000 to 105,000, Hart claimed the greatest single event was the sale of Kern River

water rights by Tenneco West to the City of Bakersfield. A public speaker of note, Mayor Hart actively promoted Bakersfield to groups seeking a location for conventions.

It was during Hart's term in the early 1970s that the "Try Kern County First" campaign (an effort to urge consumers to buy products within the county), after months of promotion, finally began to pay off. Spendable income was reported to be up by some 3.4 percent, coupled with an increase in taxable sales of 7 percent. Another indication of growth came in 1976 with the announcement of plans for a new convention hotel, to complement the civic auditorium. The proposal included a facility of 15 stories made up of hotel rooms, offices, and additional retail shop space. Civic leaders agreed that this would advance Bakersfield as a leader in West Coast tourism and more visitors would follow.

In the final quarter of 1976, Bakersfield remained the least expensive place in which a

Tenneco West played a major part in the modern development of what was originally Lloyd Tevis and James B. Haggin's Kern County Land Company property. Photo by Gregory Iger

California family could live. A 12-city survey, conducted by the American Chamber of Commerce Researchers Association, found Bakersfield residents had the lowest costs for food, transportation, utilities, health care, and miscellaneous services. The other cities surveyed had similar facilities, but Bakersfield was ranked number one among them all.

With this hearty and healthy recommendation, construction began to boom in Bakersfield. One addition was the Christian Towers, an imposing senior citizens' apartment building erected in the city's southern sector. Construction had begun on San Joaquin Community Hospital's new facility in 1973. The activity spread soon to include the building of the Rio Bravo Tennis Ranch, the Stockdale Village Shopping Center, and the Anheuser Busch plant. By 1979 a correspondent industrial construction boom climaxed with the development of Tenneco's Stockdale Industrial Park in southwest Bakersfield.

The decade ended on an upbeat note as Bakersfield continued to grow and no decline was seen by Bakersfield's businesses. The dean of Cal State Bakersfield's business college, Richard S. Wallace, stated in October 1979:

The nation's economy may improve, get worse, or "move violently sideways" during the next six months. No matter. Whatever the nation's economic fate, the Bakersfield economy is going to continue its steady upward progress. This is the concensus among 52 Bakersfield business leaders.

As Bakersfield entered the 1980s, it did so under the leadership of its new mayor, Mary K. Shell. A native daughter and journalist by profession, she was elected in November 1980. She emphasized civic pride by organizing a "Beautiful Bakersfield" committee and promoted clean-up efforts throughout the city. She had a special interest in preserving Bakersfield's historic buildings and encouraged the forma-

William B. Carpenter, Fred Miller, Eva Granados, Marge Bollinger, and Richard C. Bailey were members of the 1966 Centennial Preview Day Committee. Courtesy, Kern County Museum

tion of the Historical Preservation Commission, created by the city council in 1983.

The experts disagreed as to what the future would hold for Bakersfield as they watched interest rates climb and recession take hold of the nation. Local publications had forecasted a business boom, but some local government and business leaders expected a "bust" instead. The boomers turned out to be right as the early 1980s saw extraordinary expansion of commercial building west of Oak Street on the California Avenue corridor. In March 1980 the Easton Business Complex, a local dream, was developed in southwest Bakersfield. The original 6.65 acre tract exploded into hundreds of acres of condominiums, offices, apartments, homes, warehouses, and a new financial and business center.

The year 1980 also promised growth in petroleum, the industry's pace of activity quickening. The value of real estate was showing surprising strength, restaurant revenues were increasing, and employment was steady. The medical sector had a small boom going. Public utilities, government, grocery stores, banks, transportation facilities and department stores were all reportedly

Today the site of Tom Means' 1899 discovery well is marked as a California Historical Landmark. The first commercial oil well of the Kern River field was drilled 400 feet north of this site. Photo by Gregory Iger

enjoying business as usual. There were a few signs of slowdown, however, in manufacturing, car sales, insurance businesses, and construction. But most people were still guardedly optimistic.

The oil industry continued to be healthy as Kern County's 12th oil refinery was built by Independent Valley Energy in 1981. It was not until 1982 that Bakersfield began to feel the efforts of the national recession. The decline in local prosperity was attributed to high interest rates, but people in Bakersfield were positive, and the city's economy was, overall, surprisingly strong.

By 1983 Bakersfield's economy picked up with car sales, insurance and real estate businesses, and construction and utilities leading the way. And new growth was projected in agriculture, banks, transportation,

local government, and the medical industry. The future appeared even brighter in Bakersfield not only in mining, cattle, sheep, farming, oil, commerce, science, recreation, education, and the military, but also in new fields such as high technology, attracted to the southern San Joaquin Valley by its favorable climate and geography. The future of Bakersfield, no doubt, will be as inspiring and as rewarding as its colorful past.

Since Don Padre Fages led his men down the grapevine into the southern San Joaquin Valley in 1772, history has been made, and is continuing to be recorded, here in the heart of California's Golden Empire. The final segment in Bakersfield's history will be written by its people—people from all walks of life who find this spirited city a fine place in which to work and to live.

Previous page, above, and facing page: The foothills of the Sierra Nevada surround Kern County and Bakersfield with scenic wonders. The hills and meadows are often covered with wildflowers and California Golden Poppies.

All color photography by Gregory Iger

A Kern County almond orchard in bloom aptly symbolizes the area's agricultural richness. Almonds from Kern County are shipped worldwide.

The Kern River (left) and
the Greenhorn Mountains
(below) are two of the
geographical features that
challenged early explorers
and settlers.

Kern County's resources
include much rangeland
for livestock grazing.

Reminders of the earlier
residents of the San
Joaquin Valley, these
pictographs are on
Canebrake Creek near
Walker's Pass. Photo by
Dr. John Cawley

Sheep still graze in the county's fertile valleys as they did in the days of the first settlers.

Cotton has long been Kern County's leading agricultural crop.

Citrus fruit and grapes thrive in Kern County's mild climate. Both are important parts of the county's agricultural economy.

Facing page: A rose festival is held each year in Wasco to celebrate Kern County's status as a rose producer.

113

Kern County oil accounts for 60% of California's petroleum production. This pumping unit and refinery contribute to that output.

Whitewater kayaking, rafting, and horseback riding are some of the many outdoor activities that are enjoyed in Kern County.

Facing page: Palm trees in Bakersfield stand silhouetted against the late afternoon sun.

Bakersfield residents appreciate the delicate architectural detail of the past. There are currently many projects underway to save historic buildings.

Above: Pictured here is an ornamental detail from one of Bakersfield's historic buildings.

As both living and working space, modern architecture also has found a prominent place in Bakersfield.

The Partners

IN PROGRESS

By Howie Wines

Always looking to the future while reflecting on the past, Bakersfield and Kern County provide a healthy environment for economic progress.

History, with all its vagueness, cannot reveal exactly what was in the minds of the gentle Yowlumne tribe of the Yokuts Indians as they observed strange-appearing men invading the hunting, fishing, and gathering areas of their domain.

"Hello" or "Welcome"? Unlikely. "Keep going, stranger," was more probably the whispered and furtive plea of those proprietors of the sparse area located between today's Santa Fe Depot and Mercy Hospital.

The Indian Rancheria of Woilu, containing humble tule-and-willow dwellings, was home to these early settlers who wished nothing more than to be left alone to continue with their tribal customs. It was not to be.

The white man, in his earnest desire for adventure, exploration, religion, and other motivations, persisted in his march into the wilderness these Indians had conquered centuries before. While Kern Island in the 1860s was a 160-acre swamp with stands of willow, cottonwood, and sycamore trees, hospitality and safety were to be found in Colonel Thomas Baker's alfalfa field nearby.

Also nearby the Yokuts Indians, now relegated to a status of insignificance, watched as their tribal customs and traditions slowly evaporated into memories. Thus, then, is the march of time and of people.

Gone were the tule-and-willow dwellings. In their stead substantial buildings of wood, stone, and brick arose to form the downtown business section of Bakersfield. In 1889 the economic base of the city was bounded on the north by 20th Street and on the south by 17th Street. The east and west boundaries were "M" Street and Eye Street, respectively.

A devastating fire swept this area on July 8, 1889, leaving only Scribner's water tower—located on the southeast corner of 17th and Chester.

The community's early citizens were challenged often with adversity. Fire, flood, drought, and movements of the earth could not deter the dreamers, planners, promoters, speculators, builders, and others with energy, determination, and ingenuity.

Bakersfield emerged, time and again, stronger than before. An influx of people, capital, and the desire to succeed boosted the commercial growth of the city and its surrounding area.

Development has accelerated—and pride is reflected in the mirrored buildings that house enterprise, imagination, and citizens who have a special affection for their neighborhood.

Bakersfield's partners in progress exemplify warm civic self-esteem as their business and agricultural community continues a commitment to the growth and well-being of the city and its residents. Old dreams, yet new in commercial success and business prosperity, are a part of the proud tradition of Bakersfield.

On the following pages you will read varying accounts of a thriving combination of business and industry, government, education, culture, and people joined with prominent memories of Bakersfield's history.

GREATER BAKERSFIELD CHAMBER OF COMMERCE

The Bakersfield Civic Commercial Association held its first board of directors' meeting on November 26, 1920, officiated by president Louis Olcese, vice-president C.W. Newbery, and treasurer Arthur S. Crites.

Important early projects of the association—whose first home was two rooms in the George Hay Building—were appropriation of funds to alleviate flood conditions,

Business Bureau. The association successfully campaigned for an amendment to the city charter that established a city manager form of government.

Concentrating on "Selling the Nation's Newest City" during the early 1950s, the Chamber assisted in a nationwide NBC broadcast and articles in national publications publicizing Bakersfield.

In September 1970 the Chamber purchased and moved into new quarters at 1807 19th Street. During that decade it played an influential part in spearheading public protest to persuade the county board of supervisors to hold the line on the county tax rate, maintaining close contact with state and national legislative representatives, and offering constructive recommendations

housing needs, taxation to effect a more efficient government, highways, parks, education, economic development, and transportation.

On February 10, 1933, members voted unanimously in favor of changing the name of the expanding organization to the Bakersfield Chamber of Commerce. Relocating its offices several times during the decade, the Chamber had as its objectives at that time city-limit signs, a sewage-treatment plant, storm sewers, adequate street signs, improved postal services, and elimination of the grade crossings on the Santa Fe Railroad tracks.

In the early 1940s a staff of four directed Chamber committees, retail promotions of the retail division, a convention department, and a Better

Since December 1980 these spacious quarters at 1000 Truxtun Avenue, Suite C, have provided the Chamber with adequate facilities, which are also shared by the Convention Bureau and the Trade Club.

The earthquake of 1952 prompted another move—to the basement of the Haberfelde Building. There the Chamber remained until the following year when it moved its headquarters to 2401 L Street.

Water, employment, and higher education were prominent on the Chamber's priority lists during the 1960s. The Civic Auditorium, a project the organization had supported for many years, opened to accommodate conventions, trade shows, sports events, and cultural and recreational activities—adding much-needed job opportunities for the growing community.

for economy in school operations.

A new management philosophy evolved in 1980 to put the organization more in line with the course charted by the Chamber of Commerce of the United States. In addition to continuing to monitor local, state, and national issues, the Chamber sought ways to revitalize downtown Bakersfield through redevelopment projects, encourage the development of a downtown transit facility, and promote a metropolitan planning concept for the entire Bakersfield area.

Today the Greater Bakersfield Chamber of Commerce is a dynamic force for change in the community and the catalyst for bringing about a three-way partnership between the political, residential, and business communities.

SHELL CALIFORNIA PRODUCTION INC.

The new headquarters of Shell California Production Inc. is in the Stockdale Corporate Tower, located at the corner of Mohawk and California Avenue.

Early Shell operations included construction of a distribution terminal at Martinez, shown here in a photo taken about 1915.

Headlines throughout the country exclaimed, "The largest commercial acquisition in U.S. corporate history" in 1979 when Shell Oil Company purchased little-known Belridge Oil Company for $3.65 billion. The properties included in the purchase are located about 40 miles west of Bakersfield near McKittrick and consist of approximately 35,000 acres. With the Belridge acquisition, Shell increased its net proved domestic crude oil reserves by 44 percent and reaffirmed its long-standing interest in California—the state containing some of the deepest roots of the company's American heritage.

Even though preliminary operations started a year earlier, Shell formed the American Gasoline Company in 1912 to market imported motor fuel in the Pacific Northwest and San Francisco Bay areas. Oil production was added the following year with the acquisition of a major interest in the Coalinga field in Fresno County for $13 million. A pipeline was subsequently built from Coalinga to Martinez, where a refinery was completed in 1915.

Following the discovery by Shell of the Signal Hill field at Long Beach in 1921, the company completed a refinery at Wilmington in 1923 and began marketing activities in Southern California. Since then, Shell has pursued aggressive exploration and production efforts to furnish feedstocks for these and other operations.

For example, Shell brought in the Mount Poso field in Kern County in 1926 and discovered Ten Section a decade later. With many innovative operations being added during ensuing years, the company's producing properties now extend from the Beta field off Huntington Beach to the Sacramento gas fields. Included are properties at Kern River, Midway-Sunset, and Yorba Linda, where Shell in the 1960s pioneered the steam soak process to produce heavy oil commonly found in California.

In 1982 a restructuring of segments of Shell's exploration and production operation resulted in the creation of Shell California Production Inc., a subsidiary formed to operate all the company's producing operations in California.

The Stockdale Corporate Tower in Bakersfield now houses the corporate headquarters of SCPI. In mid-1983 employees were relocated from Houston, Texas, and Ventura to the newly constructed facility. Local employees were formerly situated a short distance away in the California Triangle Building.

SCPI employs about 1,450 people in California. There are 540 professional and support staff in Bakersfield with several hundred staff and operating personnel at various other locations in Kern County.

The relocation to Bakersfield provides senior management representation in California and enhances SCPI's efforts to manage its resources. SCPI's California oil production in 1982 averaged 160,000 barrels per day, more than one-third of the parent Shell Oil Company's domestic oil and condensate production of 443,000 barrels per day for the same period.

Shell is certainly no newcomer to the Bakersfield area, having opened its first operations office there as early as 1924. With a strong position in proved crude oil reserves, Shell, through its SCPI subsidiary, promises to continue being a partner in the community well into the 21st century.

J.L. DENIO, INC.

In 1946 Taft-born Justin L. Denio started hauling potatoes on a new Chevy two-ton flatbed truck.

Operating out of his home on Oregon Street, east of Sterling Road, Denio soon expanded his business and added a skip loader and a dump truck. Being complimented on his dependable, hard-working attitude, he earned the comment, "You're really on the ball, Justin," and made it his trademark. Business flourished, and in 1965 the operation was moved to 4208 Rosedale Highway. (Immediate plans call for another relocation to a new, larger facility in the greater Bakersfield area.)

While supervising the rebuilding of a U.S. Forest Service road near Big Bear Lake in San Bernardino County, 48-year-old Justin Denio was killed in October 1970 when a skip loader he was operating rolled over. At that time son Dale was a mechanical engineer for the Guy F. Atkinson Construction Company of South San Francisco and was working on the Mica Dam project, Columbia River, British Columbia; consequently his uncle, Melvin Denio, directed the business until Dale was named general manager in January 1974. His mother Florence, who had handled the bookkeeping chores from the beginning, continued to do so until 1979. (In her "spare time" she had raised Dale and his three sisters.)

The company, which has participated in major construction projects varying from apartment complexes in San Diego to campground facilities at Lake Tahoe, lists among its local accomplishments the primary excavation for the Bank of America Building at Truxtun and Chester avenues; the site work for the Getty-Mohawk refinery near Rosedale and Fruitvale avenues, a $60-million construction project; grading, paving, and curbs for the Guarantee Savings financial center on California Avenue; site work for several buildings at Cal State Bakersfield; grading and paving for a new gas plant in Elk Hills and the Highlands Mobile Home Park on Niles Street near Hillcrest Memorial Park; and grading, paving, conduit pipes, and utility installations for the Rio Bravo Golf Course as general contractor.

Von's markets located at Mt. Vernon and Columbus and on Wilson Road.

With 75 employees, an annual payroll of approximately $1.6 million, and a comprehensive fleet of large earth-moving and

Justin L. Denio, founder of J.L. Denio, Inc.

Dale's wife Sarah and their young children, Krista, Debbie, and Matthew, shop at Von's markets— whose facilities were prepared by J.L. Denio, Inc. The firm performed the site grading and fill, and contracted the concrete curbs, gutters, and asphalt paving for the Stockdale Center close to their home, as well as similar construction work for the

J.L. Denio, Inc., performing excavation and site work for the Bank of America construction project at Truxtun and Chester avenues. It was Bakersfield's first high-rise building.

related equipment, J.L. Denio, Inc., is still expanding.

Founder Justin L. Denio certainly was "on the ball" when he picked his company's slogan.

RIO BRAVO RESORT

Rio Bravo has developed into one of the finest resort areas in Central California. Besides its award-winning lodge and dining room, luxury condominiums, townhouses, and single-family dwellings also are part of the development.

Nearby are rafting, swimming, canoeing, tubing, and kayaking facilities on the Kern River.

Rio Bravo's tennis club, rated by Tennis Magazine as one of the top 10 facilities in the nation, hosts the annual Grand Masters Tournament.

More than 200 years ago the 16,000 acres of gently rolling hills at the base of the Sierra Nevada were part of "Father Francisco Garces country." Could the good padre have imagined the present-day Rio Bravo Resort bordering the Kern River?

George Nickel, Jr. (the great-grandson of Henry Miller, who founded Miller and Lux, Inc., and was known as the "cattle king"), also had dreams and plans. He and his dedicated staff of family and friends initiated an enterprise that has developed into Central California's finest resort area. Rio Bravo—whose lodge, with 112 spacious rooms, and dining room both received the highly coveted Four Diamond Award from the Southern California Automobile Association—is the 26th-highest-rated resort area in the country, according to Restaurant Hospitality Magazine.

Luxury condominiums as well as townhouses and single-family dwellings are part of the development, which is adjacent to the California Living Museum (CALM). Featuring a superb aviary and indigenous Kern wildlife, CALM is a special interest of Adele "Dodo" Nickel.

Rio Bravo's tennis club, rated by Tennis Magazine as one of the top 10 facilities in the nation, boasts 19 championship courts that host the annual Grand Masters Tournament. A championship 7,100-yard golf course—designed by noted architect Robert Muir Graves—is in full operation, complemented by a magnificent clubhouse. Continuing strong support is given to a proposed 15-field international soccer facility located on adjoining Rio Bravo.

Additional features of the resort include an equestrian center, which provides for boarding stables and regulation show and warm-up rings, as well as hot-air balloon rides and a

4,000-foot airstrip indicative of the up, up, and away future of Rio Bravo.

Also nearby are swimming, tubing, rafting, canoeing, and kayaking facilities on the Kern River. (The U.S. National Whitewater Championships were hosted by Rio Bravo there in 1980.) Water skiing and sailing are enjoyed on the adjacent 110-acre Lake Ming.

A native San Franciscan and a 1939 graduate of the University of California at Berkeley, Nickel became involved in the family ranch interests, and soon was responsible for all agricultural and engineering land-development operations. Under his leadership the family's 30,000-acre Buena Vista Lake property was converted from an inefficient reservoir area to one of the finest ranches in California.

However, the roots of his dream were planted in 1965, when he purchased the Rio Bravo property from the heirs of Bakersfield pioneer Louis V. Olcese. Dedicated to realizing his dream, Nickel relates: "I believe the Rio Bravo area is not only a beautiful place to live and work but that it will become one of the top resorts in California. I am dedicated to bringing this about."

WALLY TUCKER DATSUN

"Howdy, Sheriff!" is a familiar greeting in the West. In Bakersfield the greeting could be directed to former sheriffs Charles Dodge or Al Loustalot or to the present sheriff, Larry Kleier.

The salutation also would be appropriate for Wally Tucker, the unelected, but very popular, "Sheriff of Datsun Country." His advertising consultant, the late George Day (Daisa) suggested the "good guy" western approach a few years ago, and Wally has been using this theme ever since.

In 1936 the enterprising young man hitchhiked to Bakersfield from his Texas home, determined to establish his own business. He worked as a mechanic for 11 years at the Bakersfield Garage, and with the help of his wife Eleanor saved frugally toward reaching that goal; as a result, Tucker Autos became a reality in 1947. With just over $1,000 Wally opened his fledgling operation on a vacant lot at the corner of 19th and Baker streets, offering three choice used cars.

Billy Eddington was hired as mechanic in 1949 to help make certain the vehicles could be driven off the lot; he is still employed at Tucker Datsun, and is still making sure that the customer is pleased and satisfied with his new or used car. Wally's brother Dick joined the firm in 1952 and retired in 1981 after 29 years of service.

When the entrepreneur decided to

Until 1959 Wally Tucker Datsun sold only used cars at its 19th and Baker streets location.

become a factory distributor early in 1959, there were nine European-franchise opportunities available; however, following his banker's advice, he chose none of them. Instead, he drove to Los Angeles in his finest used car—and became the second Datsun dealer in the United States. (San Diego Datsun had signed a few weeks earlier.)

Wally Tucker Datsun is regularly listed as one of the top Datsun dealers in the United States. Receiving the *Time* magazine Quality Dealer and the National Automobile Dealers' Association Award in 1971, the founder was one of 71 so honored from 22,000 candidates.

The featured story in *Bakersfield*

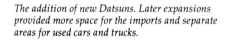

The addition of new Datsuns. Later expansions provided more space for the imports and separate areas for used cars and trucks.

Lifestyle in May 1982, the "sheriff" was asked by publisher-writer Steve Walsh about his business philosophy. Wally responded:

"It's very important to hire the right kind of person. You must look for someone who wants to work, who wants to do the job, someone who is dedicated toward improvement. Without that kind of person your business just won't go any-where. I invest in my employees and I invest in my customers—the people of Bakersfield who have been good to me."

In return, Wally has been good to the people of Bakersfield, and to the many organizations and charities he has helped sponsor or found.

In February 1978 Lee Sattley was brought into the business as vice-president/general manager of Wally Tucker Datsun. In 1978 Sattley became a partner and oversees the daily operations of the now very diversified business.

Wally and Eleanor have made their home in East Bakersfield throughout their 42 years of marriage. After 36 years in business Wally is semi-retired but looks forward to his many activities.

BAKERSFIELD SANDSTONE BRICK COMPANY

In 1886 James Curran purchased 40 acres and established the Bakersfield Sandstone Brick Company. It has served the Bakersfield community from the same location ever since.

The torrid Sunday on July 8, 1889, in Bakersfield found flags and bunting from the celebration on the Fourth still draping the porches and buildings along the parade route. Although church services and relaxing holiday picnics were scheduled, an ominous cloud of smoke that suddenly arose over downtown Bakersfield would change all plans. It was the big fire of 1889—and in its wake the only downtown structure left standing was Scribner's Water Tower.

The few lean-tos and tents that sprang up afterward soon were replaced by brick from James Curran's brickyard, which he had founded only three years earlier on East Truxtun Avenue.

Curran, who had learned his brick-making craft from his father back in Dixon, Illinois, joined the westward movement following a doctor's orders to "Go west, young man, and your asthma will be better." His travels ended in Bakersfield in 1886 where, at the age of 24, he purchased 40 acres for his future business. Today's Bakersfield Sandstone Brick Company is still located on this site.

The "Curran touch" was present in the early days just as it is today. Well-known structures such as the original Beale Memorial Clock Tower (one original Sandstone brick still can be observed about two-thirds up the west side of the 1964-rebuilt clock tower, presently located at the Kern County Museum), St. Francis Catholic Church, Bakersfield Garage, the Tegler Hotel, the Scribner Opera House, and the first Standard Oil Building grew from Sandstone materials.

In 1919 the firm moved into lumber and lumber products, and in 1928 added a complete hardware department. By 1959 the sale of brick had become such a small part of the company operations that the manufacture of brick was discontinued. Instituting the equipment-rental division in 1965, Sandstone since has expanded into construction loans and land development through the formation of the Ace Financial Corporation.

A major fire destroyed most of the office, store, and warehouse facilities in November 1978, but from those ashes arose a new home facing Truxtun Avenue. Today's operation includes a nursery, home-decorating center, and a railroad dining car, as well as a full-line contractor, lumber sale yard, and truss-manufacturing plant.

Since World War II leadership of the company primarily has been under the direction of James Curran II and Walter F. Heisey, both of whom actively participate in Bakersfield's community affairs. Curran, president of Sandstone, is a grandson of the founder; Heisey (a retired U.S. Navy Reserve Captain) serves as vice-president of Sandstone and the Curran Corporation, and is president of Ace Financial Corporation. He also is a former vice-mayor and city councilman.

Bakersfield Sandstone Brick Company helped rebuild its community in 1889; it is now building for the future of a dynamic Bakersfield and Kern County, through its direction of continued growth, expanded services, and new innovating opportunities.

James Curran II, president (left), and Walter F. Heisey, vice-president, in front of Sandstone's national award-winning "Home Center of the Year."

BROCK'S DEPARTMENT STORE

Brock's Department Store, now celebrating its 84th anniversary, is one of the leading retail establishments in Bakersfield, despite its having suffered earthquakes, fires, and an onslaught of competitive enterprises.

The story begins with the founding of a retail venture in Willows, California, by two brothers, Moses and Amiel Hochheimer, who opened three stores in Glenn County beginning in 1876.

The fledgling venture suffered its first of many setbacks when it was barely six years old. On May 30, 1882, a fire broke out at two o'clock in the morning in Willows, and the principal business portion of town was quickly reduced to ashes. Because there were no organized facilities for fighting fires at that time, citizens were compelled to stand by helplessly as their property was destroyed. Among those burned down was the young firm of Hochheimer and Company. Undaunted by their setback, the brothers rebuilt their store, only to

see it destroyed by a similar blaze in 1886.

Following this catastrophic conflagration, Hochheimer and Company was rebuilt along with the rest of the business section of town, and in 1887 the Willows Water and Light Company was incorporated. With the installation of the firm's pumps and tanks, the local fire menace was materially reduced.

The brothers purchased a store in Bakersfield in 1900. It was a one-room building located on the east side of Chester Avenue just north of the alley between 19th and 20th streets.

Hochheimer and Company assumed control of Belau's Pioneer Store (established as the Pioneer Store by Dave Hirshfeld in 1890) on

September 20, 1900. At that time, the population of Bakersfield was between 5,500 and 6,000 people.

The concern pledged to augment the stock of merchandise which already consisted of agricultural implements, boots and shoes, carriages and wagons, clothing, dry goods, and groceries. The brothers wanted to make a bid for a fair share of the patronage of the people of Bakersfield and Kern County. To do so necessitated an enlargement of the physical facilities, which had not changed since the building's construction in 1890.

An immediate remodeling of the storefront and the addition of a second story were undertaken. The storefront was changed from a couple of display windows and four sets of

The original Pioneer Store, forerunner of today's Brock's Department Store, was established in 1890 by Dave Hirshfeld. Situated on the east side of Chester Avenue between 19th and 20th streets, it was the first business building in Bakersfield to have electric lights.

While its store was being renovated, reinforced, and enlarged following the 1952 earthquakes, Brock's occupied two circus tents which were erected on a parking lot in the Westchester area. The store did business in this fashion for approximately nine months.

recessed doors to one main entrance flanked by large show windows which extended along the rest of the Chester Avenue frontage. These major alterations were completed in 1901. No significant alterations were made to the exterior of this building for the next 18 years.

The man for whom the present business is named—Malcolm Brock—was the nephew of the two

Hochheimer brothers, and he worked for them in Glenn County beginning in 1894. He worked there until 1906 when he returned to San Francisco, his birthplace. In 1908 he went to Alaska to establish banks and mercantile stores in Cordova and Valdez. John Brock, Sr., presently chairman of the board, and his sister Betty were born in Alaska.

In 1919, while the Bakersfield store was managed by Ira and Monroe Homer, sons of Amiel Hochheimer (the family name was shortened from Hochheimer to Homer in 1918), it was totally devastated by a fire. A completely new store was erected at Chester Avenue and 20th Street to replace it in 1920.

At this time, Malcolm Brock and his wife Aileen were living in Cordova, Alaska, where he had become president of both the Blum-O'Neill Company and the First Bank of Cordova. Envisioning a dim future in Alaska, however, he sold out his interests there and returned to California in 1922, at which time he

was persuaded by the Homers to become manager of the Bakersfield operation. Two years later Brock purchased the store from the Homers and formed the Malcolm Brock Company.

The business was run by Malcolm Brock and Monroe Homer, Sr. John M. Brock came aboard in 1938 and they were assisted by Monroe Homer, Jr., who joined the firm in 1945. The senior Homer passed away in 1951.

The Tehachapi-Bakersfield earthquakes in 1952 severely damaged the Brock building, forcing the store to operate from two circus tents erected in Westchester. At that time, a nearby facility was leased from actress Ann Sheridan in order to accommodate a line of better women's ready-to-wear. This establishment became Brock's Westchester, noted for its reputation of featuring women's couturier designs. The downtown Bakersfield store, meanwhile, was reinforced, remodeled, and enlarged. In 1953 the company moved from the circus tents back to the 20th and Chester location.

Brock's expanded along with Bakersfield, establishing the Valley Plaza store in 1967 and becoming one of the anchors of that shopping center.

Malcolm Brock passed away in

1962 and the reins were turned over to John M. Brock, son of Malcolm and Aileen, and to Monroe Homer, Jr., son of Monroe Homer, Sr., and Clara Homer and grandson of Amiel Hochheimer. Aileen Brock died in 1977 at the age of 91.

In the family-owned and -operated tradition, Brock's continues to grow and currently has plans for expansion. John Sr. is chairman of the board; John Jr. is president and chief executive officer; Bill Colm, son of Betty Brock Colm and grandson of Malcolm Brock, is executive vice-president. Also involved in the business are Steve Homer, son of Monroe Homer, Jr., and his sister, Gail Homer Jenkins. Marti Brock, sister of John Brock, Jr., is also a part of the concern.

The Lori Brock Junior Museum at Pioneer Village was named after the daughter of John Brock, Sr., and Gladys Brock. Lori Brock was killed in a traffic accident in 1972.

After more than a century since its beginning in Willows, California, Brock's Department Store is respected as a Bakersfield tradition.

Hochheimer and Company's new Bakersfield store as it appeared following reconstruction caused by the fire of August 22, 1919. The building retained this appearance until the earthquakes of 1952, which weakened the structure and necessitated the filling in of all the windows on the upper two floors.

Following the 1952 earthquakes, Brock's downtown store was refurbished and enlarged. As depicted in this 1960s photo, its appearance has not changed much to the present day.

LUFKIN'S BUSINESS COLLEGE

In celebration of Kern County's 100th anniversary, the *Kern County Centennial Almanac* was published in 1966. In a chronological listing of "Historical Events of Significance," the year 1907 called attention to the establishment of "a Bakersfield Business College."

That institution was Lufkin's Business College, which was located over the Kern Printing Company in a building near 21st and Eye streets. Lufkin's filled a need in the Bakersfield community by offering secretarial and accounting courses, and boasted an average attendance of 45 to 50 students.

From 1908 until 1979 the school was located at 1304 L Street. Harry Lufkin designed and constructed the 1,800-square-foot facility and built a small home next door for himself and his wife.

occupies a new building in the Westwind Business Park.

In the interim Erin Middleton, a former teacher at the college, and

Lufkin's Business College was located in this building at 1304 L Street from 1908 to 1979.

in 1975 following Cromwell's death.

Lufkin's continues to be highly respected academically, with its graduates comprising some of Bakersfield's most prominent business people. Its staff of three in 1975 has grown to 10, serving 120 to

Lufkin's moved to a larger facility at 405 South Chester in 1979. This 3,300-square-foot center housed the college until 1981, when the present owners, Dwight and Laura Danley, decided to enlarge. They remodeled and occupied a larger facility at 500 Baker Street from 1981 to February 1984. Lufkin's now

Today Lufkin's Business College occupies this new facility in the Westwind Business Park at 1800 Westwind Drive.

Dale Ludwick had purchased the enterprise from Harry Lufkin in 1952. They operated it until 1966, when Forrest W. Cromwell purchased it. The Danleys took over

160 students each year.

The business college specializes in vocational training, with concentration on specific areas of student interest and community needs. Current courses offer training to equip students to perform as receptionists, clerk-typists, and full-charge bookkeepers. Junior accounting and general secretarial areas of study, both legal and medical, also are part of the curriculum. Modern equipment includes electric IBM and Royal typewriters, electronic printing calculators, and word-processing and data-processing units.

Lufkin's offers tuition scholarships to local high schools each year. The awards, valued at more than $20,000, are presented to deserving students chosen by the scholarship committees of the schools, with the finalists being selected by the Business and Education Committee of the Greater Bakersfield Chamber of Commerce.

TENNECO WEST

The West is a chapter in time pulling remarkable men over the next mountain, where the sun always turns to gold. In the late 1850s two such remarkable men, Lloyd Tevis and James Ben Ali Haggin, began to reclaim the southern end of California's San Joaquin Valley.

While they hoped to attract settlers to the opportunities of California farming, the land that was a summer desert and a winter swamp somewhat obscured the settlers' view of this opportunity. Undaunted, the two men built a flood-control system to put the Kern River to work, then dug irrigation ditches that turned thousands of acres into rich grazing land. By the 1890s settlers began to see the real opportunity and started farming the land.

The Tevis-Haggin properties became the Kern County Land Company, and for the next 30 years continued to graze cattle, grow and market crops, and develop water rights as well as irrigation know-how. Then, as if water weren't enough, they found "black gold."

A world war came and went, while oil earnings went back into the business developing more land, cultivating more acreage, and building modern processing and packaging plants.

In 1959 the company acquired Walker Manufacturing, a leading producer of automotive equipment; and in 1964 Case became part of the corporate family. (J.I. Case is a world leader in the manufacture of construction and farm equipment.)

Finally, in 1967, Tenneco, Inc., acquired the Kern County Land Company; three years later that name was retired, becoming Tenneco West. To manage its operations most effectively, the firm is divided into three divisions: land management, fresh products, and processed foods.

Land management is responsible for Tenneco's investment in 1.1 million acres of property in Arizona and California, which includes the 100,000-acre San Emidio Ranch south of Bakersfield. A good example of land management is Stockdale, whose 6,000 acres of previous desert is now home to thousands in Bakersfield.

With an eye to the future, the corporation donated 370 acres for the construction of California State College, Bakersfield, which currently has 3,000 full-time students.

Pursuant to the task of Tenneco West's fresh products division to meet an increasing demand for the very best of fruits and vegetables year-round, the firm boasts one of the largest packing and cold-storage facilities in the world—eight acres under one roof—in the headquarters city of Bakersfield. A nearby 5,100-

The Kern County Land Company, circa 1885.

acre facility provides much of the volume that makes the organization one of the largest table grape shippers in America.

The third and most rapidly growing division of Tenneco West is processed foods, focusing primarily on almonds, raisins, pistachios, and dates. The company's "Sun Giant" products are among the leading national brands.

Additionally, Tenneco West is carrying on its legacy of innovation, diversity, and enterprise, and building a major new business nationwide in the retailing of dried fruits, nuts, and related products through its House of Almonds specialty store chain.

The new Tenneco West office building, located on Ming Avenue, Bakersfield, was constructed in 1983.

CALCOT, LTD.

On a cold February day in 1927, a group of 21 cotton farmers met in Delano, California, to found the cotton marketing cooperative that would eventually come to be known as Calcot, Ltd. In starting the new organization, they didn't feel they were shooting for the moon; they were just looking for a way to gain more value for their cotton.

From that start over 55 years ago, Calcot, Ltd., has grown to be one of the most successful cotton marketing cooperatives in the United States. A loyal membership of over 3,300 cotton growers in California and Arizona, a professional marketing staff, support from grower-owned gins, and the finest facilities available have all contributed to making Calcot a leading marketer of cotton worldwide.

By 1929 the San Joaquin Cotton Growers cooperative was already making organizational changes. It acquired the new name of California Cotton Cooperative Association, and brought in a professional cotton marketer, Clarence C. Seldon, to handle the members' cotton. Seldon's arrival, however, came at the same time the country was starting to sink deeper into its greatest economic depression, and cotton prices fell to record lows of less than six cents a pound.

Rough times lay ahead for the cooperative. It wasn't just the Great Depression that was ailing the CCCA. There were trials and errors in the cooperative, the testing in the fire that all new movements and ideas must go through, but the CCCA hung on.

In 1932, in an effort to gain more warehousing facilities and office space, the CCCA moved from Delano to Bakersfield. From 1933 to 1968 cotton grower L.W. Frick served as leader of the board of directors. By 1943 the board had decided that its

Thomas W. Smith has been president of Calcot's 3,300-member cooperative since 1977.

struggling but tenacious organization needed a change in its management, a change that would bring stability to the cooperative.

Frick was given the task of finding a new manager, and his search resulted in the discovery of a man who would later be given the major credit for the successful development of Calcot, Ltd. His name was J. Russell Kennedy.

Kennedy, a bright young man from Texas who had distinguished himself in the USDA, proposed radical changes for the foundering organization. Among those changes was the stipulation that the newly named Calcot, Ltd., would no longer purchase cotton on the open market or from growers, but instead would concentrate on marketing the cotton harvested by its members.

If the plan didn't work, Kennedy said, the association would be discontinued at no further loss to the membership. But the idea did catch on under the strong leadership of Kennedy. Stronger operations, a growing membership, and a newly

developed cotton seed called the San Joaquin Valley Acala variety all helped Calcot flourish.

During the late '40s and '50s Calcot grew at a tremendous rate, and in 1955 the group welcomed growers from Arizona into its membership. Strong support from Far West growers enabled Calcot to develop a vigorous role in the marketplace, not only in the United States but also in the world market.

In 1973 Calcot became the first U.S. cotton company to directly negotiate a sale with the People's Republic of China. Egypt and Eastern Europe were other major markets that were opened to receive Calcot cotton to fill their cotton needs.

The history of Calcot is woven with the names of outstanding leaders such as Kennedy, Seldon, Frick, William McFarlane, and G.L. "Sam" Seitz (who joined Calcot under Kennedy and later became president). Harold C. Weeth, chairman of the 61-member board of directors, and current Calcot president Thomas W. Smith retain the pioneer spirit of the original 21 farmers who met on that cold February day in 1927.

SAN JOAQUIN COMMUNITY HOSPITAL

In Bakersfield today there is a hospital committed to creating less need for health care services. How did the city come to have a hospital that sees its mission as preventive as much as curative?

San Joaquin Community Hospital has been serving the Bakersfield community for more than 70 years. Many changes have taken place since the hospital's modest beginning in 1910 at the northwest corner of 27th and Eye streets.

Margaret Quinn and Mary O'Donnell designed the original three-story structure, which featured the most up-to-date nursing facilities and was an early landmark, noted for its attractive, spacious piazzas.

The first home of the San Joaquin Community Hospital, located at the northwest corner of 27th and Eye streets, was an early landmark, noted for its attractive, spacious piazzas.

For a time San Joaquin Community Hospital operated as a for-profit institution, but in 1964 Dr. Joseph Smith, the owner, had a vision that greater good would come to the community if the hospital were donated to a nonprofit corporation. He specified that the institution be managed by members of the Seventh-day Adventist Church. A dedicated

group of Adventist physicians and lay people formed the San Joaquin Community Hospital Corporation and accepted the challenge to serve the community not only by treating ills, but also by providing education for the prevention of disease.

The hospital facilities were expanded in 1957 to include 18 more beds and three modern operating rooms. In 1971 Dr. Neil Arbegast, assisted by Dr. Marion Barnard, pioneered the first open-heart surgery program in Kern County. In March 1973 Dr. Michael DeBakey, world-renowned heart surgeon, came to Bakersfield as the guest speaker for the dedication of the new 166-bed hospital located across the street from the original facility.

With the support of many dedicated physicians, community leaders, and loyal employees, the San Joaquin Community Hospital became one of the most advanced and modern health care centers in Kern County. Since that time the hospital has offered a broad variety of services, including one of the largest heart-catheterization programs in the state of California. A very progressive oncology program was also developed. At this writing, it is the only certified oncology program in

The present home of the San Joaquin Community Hospital is located across the street from the original facility.

Kern County.

Perhaps the most exciting development came in 1967 when the hospital recruited Dr. John Scharffenberg, a practicing physician with a master's degree in public health from Harvard University. His challenge was to develop the Community Health Education Department. This new community service department was to offer free and low-cost programs such as weight control and stop-smoking clinics, cancer prevention seminars, and classes on coronary risk reduction. The scientific studies conducted through the hospital received nationwide attention when Senator George McGovern asked Dr. Scharffenberg for input to the Senate Select Committee on Nutrition and Human Needs. The hospital, through its health education department, has been requested to present a paper before the American Association for the Advancement of Health.

Drawing on this rich history of community service, the medical staff and employees of the San Joaquin Community Hospital are dedicated not only to helping people get well, but to staying well.

KERO-TV23

It was on September 26, 1953, in the Elks Club building, on 17th Street between Chester and Eye streets, that KERO Radio was playing the popular music of the day.

Down the street, in the Spanish Ballroom of the El Tejon Hotel, television cameras, lights, a boom mike, and assorted equipment replaced tables and chairs and KERO-TV, Channel 10, was on the air.

The NBC affiliate was built and operated by the Kern County Broadcasters, Inc. Gene De Young, president of KERO Radio; his vice-president, Ed Urner; Ken Croes, for years a Bakersfield city councilman; and Ed Andress continued with double duty on the radio and TV operations. Other members of the original TV enterprise were Gordon Harlan, a Clovis rancher; Bryan Coleman of Bakersfield Savings and Loan; and Mrs. Pearl Lamert, wife of Ralph Lamert. The Lamerts worked with the Schamblin Brothers—Leo, Frank, and Charles—and in 1932 established the first television station west of the Mississippi, W6XAH. This "backyard" TV operation evolved in 1933 to become today's KPMC Radio, now owned by Dan and Mary Speare.

Ed Urner, who built KLYD Radio, also established a companion TV station—now KPWR-TV. He later purchased KERN Radio in 1966.

The local group sold KERO-TV in 1957 to Marietta Broadcasting, an outgrowth of the Wrather-Alvarez Group (owned by Jack Wrather and his actress wife, Bonita Granville).

On May 13, 1959, Transcontinent Television assumed ownership, followed by Time-Life on April 1, 1964. The present owner, McGraw-Hill Broadcasting, took over the operation on June 1, 1972.

KERO-TV developed and pioneered a remote telecast vehicle in 1957. It allowed local audiences to view Renegade football games as well as the popular "McMahan's House Party," plus other special events.

In July 1963, KERO was required to move from VHF Channel 10 to UHF Channel 23 in order to comply with federal regulations.

From its very first telecast, KERO has been number one in local news reporting. Burleigh Smith, the station's first official news director, is currently producer and co-anchor of the "The 23 News."

Smith left the station in 1960 and was replaced by Howie Wines (on

Burleigh Smith, KERO-TV's first official news director, is currently the producer and co-anchor of "The 23 News."

leave from the Kern County Sheriff's Department). Wines returned to county employment and Ken Brown was named as director of news. Burleigh has returned to KERO and over the years the following news directors have been appointed to assist on the all-important coverage of the news: Dick Jamison, Stan Redmond, Ron Moore, Steve Talbot, Ron Kilgore, Dave Halyman, Jonathan Mumm, and Walt Brown.

An unforgettable late-afternoon live program was "Cousin Herb's Trading Post." The country-western music program, hosted by Herb Henson (first manager of KUZZ Radio, now owned by Buck Owens), had regular performers such as Jimmy Thomason, Buck Owens, Cliff Crawford, Fuzzy Owen, Merle Haggard, Tommy Duncan, and Bill Woods. The afternoon movie host for 17 years was Don Rodewald.

A strong community involvement continues to mark the progress of KERO-TV. KERO Radio? That station is now KGEOldies and is playing much of the same music that was popular back in 1953.

KERO-TV23 studios and offices are located on 21st Street.

FLOYD'S STORES, INC.

You undoubtedly have heard the expression, "Your grandma wears Army boots!"

Following World War II, interest in war-surplus items played a major part in the American economy. Maybe grandma didn't actually wear Army boots but certainly the youngsters capitalized on the expression, the idea, and the bargains available at the many newly opened war-surplus stores. Lunch boxes were replaced by ammunition boxes, Army flashlights appeared in many homes, and Eisenhower jackets constituted fashionable attire to the teenagers of the 1940s.

Floyd Burcham did wear Army boots—and the 90th Infantry Division sergeant also wore a Bronze Star, Purple Heart, Presidential Unit citation, the European Theater of Operation ribbon (with four battle stars), the Good Conduct Medal, and the Combat Infantryman's badge. Released from a Daytona Beach, Florida, Army convalescent hospital in June 1946, Floyd and his bride Anne returned to the Bakersfield area where he had swamped potatoes in Shafter prior to the war. He and a friend, Pat Savage, also had operated a small hamburger haven in that same city.

In 1946 Savage and partner Sam Smiser were in the war-surplus business and Burcham quickly decided to join them. He took his

This Savage War Surplus Headquarters at 3940 Chester Avenue was purchased by Floyd Burcham in 1952. The name was changed to Floyd's and it has served as a base of operations since.

Army savings and, as half owner, opened a war-surplus store in Porterville. (The Burchams slept on surplus Army cots in back of the store.) He then opened stores in Tulare and Dinuba in 1948. Burcham sold his interest in the three stores to Savage in 1950 and continued to help run the entire operation, which now encompassed 16 stores. The Savage War Surplus Headquarters was located at 212 North Chester Avenue.

Burcham purchased the Savage store at 3940 Chester Avenue in 1952. He changed the name to Floyd's and began to establish a base of operations that to this day continues to grow and serve customers with a large variety of consumer goods. In

Floyd Burcham, shown here in 1952 flanked by Wally Holcheck (Savage War Surplus general manager) and Pat Savage.

fact, expansion over the years now includes three "True Value" Hardware stores, an office-furniture and office-designing service, and a canvas-manufacturing outlet.

A Floyd's store on Baker Street near Monterey opened in 1954; it closed in 1958 when Burcham moved the merchandise to 1884 South Chester. In 1968 he built and opened the present location at 2020 South Chester and added a nursery-garden-patio center in addition to a floral and gift shop.

A sports fan and former boxing champion, Floyd Burcham has made certain his stores are the epitome in service to the outdoor enthusiast. Guns and ammunition, fishing and camping gear, and all types of clothing and related accessories are given special attention—as is each and every customer. So-called war-surplus merchandise has long been depleted. As a substitute, this type of merchandise is brand-new, primarily manufactured in Korea and Japan.

Floyd Burcham may not wear Army boots today, but he remembers—and Bakersfield is the richer for his memories.

OCCIDENTAL EXPLORATION AND PRODUCTION COMPANY

Los Angeles-based Occidental Petroleum Corporation was organized in 1920 to explore for and produce crude oil and natural gas. Thirty-six years later Dr. Armand Hammer, retired millionaire entrepreneur, entered the scene.

Occidental was struggling to survive, with a net worth of $34,000 and shares trading at 18 cents, when Dr. Hammer put up $100,000 so it could drill two exploratory wells. He figured it was at worst a good tax shelter. Both wells came in and put Occidental back on its feet. Dr. Hammer decided that retirement wasn't for him.

By 1957 Dr. Hammer had become Occidental's largest shareholder—and its president, supervising a handful of employees. Dr. Hammer began searching for a top-notch driller, one with particular expertise in wildcatting. He learned that when the majors had drilling problems in California, they said, "Send for Gene Reid."

Eugene C. Reid grew up in the oil town of Maricopa with oil in his blood and drilling on his mind. At age 15, he was cleaning bricks and rebricking boilers on a lease in the Midway-Sunset field. In 1959 a tin-roofed shed on Pierce Road housed Gene Reid Drilling, Inc., which employed 10 people. Early that year, for $400,000 in stock, Occidental acquired Gene Reid Drilling and a staff of some of California's brightest young oil men.

One of them convinced Dr. Hammer in 1961 to shoot the works on that year's final well—in Lathrop, where some majors had already failed. Drill they did, and Occidental discovered California's second-largest gas field. The strike set a precedent for seemingly impossible achievements.

Other early California successes included Arbuckle, West Grimes, West Buttes, Mulligan Hill, Brentwood, and West Los Angeles.

In 1966 Dr. Hammer asked, "If we could go any place in the world to look for oil, where would we want to go?" Oxy's petroleum geologists answered, "Libya." King Idris granted Occidental two concessions but, three dry holes and millions of dollars later, even Gene Reid despaired: "Libya is just no place for a small company like Oxy." The next hole Oxy punched in the desert hit a large field of sweet crude—at a site abandoned by the majors. Oxy was no longer a "small company."

As drilling continued in Libya, Oxy acquired The Permian Corporation, the nation's leading independent marketer and transporter of crude oil. In 1968 Oxy added industry giants Island Creek Coal Company and Hooker Chemical Corporation to the corporate roster.

The 1970s saw Oxy's Bakersfield team again beat the oil and gas odds—in Peru, where many companies had failed, and in the British North Sea, where Oxy discovered the giant Piper field less than a year after being awarded blocks.

Since its beginning in 1959, Oxy has discovered well over five billion barrels of crude oil and operates some of the most successful exploration and production programs in the world.

Occidental acquired the nation's largest beef processor, Iowa Beef Processors, Inc, in 1981. The following year Oxy acquired Cities Service Company, thus becoming America's ninth-largest oil company and 15th-largest industrial concern.

And it all started in Bakersfield.

Occidental's first Bakersfield building, 1960. After several expansions and additions, it is still part of the present complex at 5000 Stockdale Highway.

WICKERSHAM JEWELERS

Since the turn of the century one of the most active business corners in Bakersfield has been 19th and Eye streets. The southeast corner has been the home of Wickersham Jewelers since May 1911, when the Brower Building was completed. At the store opening people from all over the valley came to see the magnificent display of fine lead crystal and 14-karat yellow-gold pocket watches.

Charles William (C.W.) Wickersham actually opened his first store in 1901 in the 1300 block of 19th Street, after which he moved to a new location at 1425 19th Street where the operation continued until February 1905. The new corporation of Wickersham, Wrenn and Staples was formed at this time. The enterprise opened a book and stationery store at 1827 Chester Avenue, the present site of Martin's Shoes and a

portion of Vest Drugs. The corporation was dissolved, with C.W. retaining the jewelry business until his death. He died while spending a weekend at his Caliente cabin in June 1916.

Gordon Wickersham, C.W.'s grandson, is president and general manager. His paternal grandmother, Maude, assumed management and was active in the business until shortly before her death in 1951.

Charles Wickersham, Gordon's uncle, entered the firm in 1923; and his father, Walter Wickersham, joined in 1924. Aunt Katherine Wickersham followed in the family footsteps in 1929. Another of Gordon Wickersham's uncles, James Walton, is past president and now semi-retired, and his sister, Janet Gillum, is secretary/treasurer.

Although the store was damaged

during the 1952 earthquake and was modernized shortly after, the original showcases of handsome polished mahogany and cut glass, installed in 1911, are still in use at Wickersham Jewelers. They reflect the history that was described in a 1914 Kern County book as a "treasure house of magnificent wares that stands out like a scintillating gem."

In November 1983 Wickersham Jewelers opened a new branch in the beautiful East Hills Shopping Mall.

Below
By 1901 the gas lights had been replaced by electric bulbs. In the center of the aisle is an electric heater. Charles William (C.W.) Wickersham is at left.

Bottom
Wickersham Jewelers is still located at 19th and Eye streets, as it was in the 1920s when this photo was taken. Walter Wickersham is second from the left.

BAKERSFIELD CALIFORNIAN

The *Bakersfield Californian* is the direct descendant of Kern County's first newspaper, the *Weekly Courier*. In April 1866 the state legislature created Kern County and made Havilah, the small mining town to which gold miners had rushed two years before, the county seat. Four months after the county's creation, George A. Tiffany, using a horse-drawn wagon, brought a press and a collection of type from San Jose to Havilah. On August 18, 1866, the first issue of the four-page *Weekly Courier* appeared. Tiffany sold the newspaper to J.K. Acklin one month later and Acklin changed the paper's name to the *Havilah Weekly Courier*. The newspaper was published in Havilah until December 1869 when, following a shift in the county's population, it moved to Bakersfield and set up shop as the *Kern County Weekly Courier*.

The *Kern County Weekly Courier* was published until 1875, the last four years in competition with another Bakersfield newspaper, the *Southern Californian*. In 1875 Julius Chester, publisher of the *Southern Californian*, bought out the *Kern County Weekly Courier*. Chester sold the newspaper to George Wear in 1878, who sold it the following year to A.C. Maude. Maude changed the paper's name to the *Kern County Californian*. By the time Maude sold the newspaper to J.M. Reuck in 1892, he had developed it into both a *Daily Californian* and a *Weekly Californian*. The following year Reuck sold both newspapers to John Isaac who, in turn, sold the papers to George Weeks. Weeks ran the *Californian* for three years, finally selling it in 1897 to a former Kern County superintendent of schools, Alfred E. Harrell.

Harrell had come to Kern County at the age of 19 to teach school in Tehachapi. At the age of 23 he was elected Kern County superintendent of schools. Upon completion of his third term he purchased the *Daily Californian*. At that time the four-page newspaper was issued in a rented room on 19th Street. Its employees included one reporter, a printer, three typesetters, a printer's "devil," and three carrier boys.

In 1901 Harrell moved the *Californian* into its own home on Eye Street between 19th and 20th streets. At that time the company's first wire service was leased and a Linotype was purchased. In 1907 Harrell rechristened the newspaper the *Bakersfield Californian*. By 1911 the newspaper was housed in a new, two-story brick building at the same location, had 44 employees, and produced editions of six to 10 pages.

Over the next 20 years the *Bakersfield Californian*, under Harrell's leadership, won over 30 state and national awards for journalistic excellence. At the time of his passing in 1946, Harrell was one of the most respected publishers in California and the nation.

The 1926 home, and present downtown location of the Bakersfield Californian —*17th and Eye streets.*

Harrell's wife Virginia directed the newspaper until her death in 1954, whereupon their daughter, Bernice Harrell Chipman, assumed control. Mrs. Chipman guided the organization until her death in 1967. Mrs. Chipman's daughter, Alfred Harrell's granddaughter, Berenice Fritts Koerber, has served as president of the *Bakersfield Californian* since that time. She and her two sons, Don and Ted Fritts, publisher and co-publisher/editor, respectively, have continued the newspaper's tradition of excellence.

The first real home for the Californian, *on Eye Street between 19th and 20th, circa 1920.*

MERCY HOSPITAL

Humble beginnings—but with continual growth—has become the symbol and representative character of Mercy Hospital.

The modest 14-bed St. Clair Hospital, founded in 1910, rapidly grew to a 50-bed hospital which was constructed on the present Truxtun Avenue site. The name was changed to Mercy Hospital in 1913.

As Bakersfield grew, so did the hospital. To meet the medical demand, the present east wing of the hospital was constructed in 1927, adding 44 more beds. Mercy continued to improve and expand its services, until by the end of World War II it offered 99 beds, with medical, surgical, and children's departments; radiology; a clinical laboratory; and emergency services.

When an earthquake struck Bakersfield in 1952, the Sisters of Mercy were faced with the necessity

Today Mercy Hospital is a 226-bed general acute care hospital with a 50-bed skilled nursing facility.

St. Clair Hospital, founded in 1910, became Mercy Hospital when this 50-bed facility was constructed on Truxtun Avenue.

of reconstructing most of the main facility. With help from the community, the present center section of the hospital was completed in 1954. A 50-bed nursing home followed in 1957, and in 1963 a 28-bed pediatric unit was constructed. The children's unit was dedicated in memory of Chester I. Meade, M.D., Bakersfield's first pediatrician.

Several years ago the administration, board of directors, and medical staff recognized the need to augment Mercy's diagnostic and treatment services. It was necessary to update the operations in order to attract highly qualified medical practitioners to the staff. The result of this endeavor is the $10-million diagnostic and treatment wing, completed in 1976.

Currently, Mercy is a 226-bed general acute care hospital with a 50-bed skilled nursing facility.

Specialized units in neurology, pediatrics, coronary care, and intensive care are now available. The hospital offers additional services such as a cardiac treatment center, hemodialysis unit, and a full-body CAT (computerized axial tomography) scanner. The physical therapy department, speech and audiology department, enterostomal services, and noninvasive cardiology unit comprise other sophisticated medical services. More than 1,200 employees, as well as volunteers, make up today's health care team at Mercy Hospital.

The two Sisters of Mercy who came to Bakersfield in 1910 were continuing the tradition of service that began in Dublin, Ireland, in 1831. From its beginning, the Order has responded to plague, famine, and strife around the world. Now 300 in number, the Sisters of Mercy have been prepared by years of spiritual formation, education, and professional training. With these qualifications, the Sisters continue to serve the needs of the people.

The present administrator, Sister Phyllis Hughes, guides her staff in this tradition of providing the highest quality health care to the Bakersfield community.

SULLIVAN'S STANDARD PETROLEUM COMPANY

Tom Sullivan left his native village of Skibbereen, South County Cork, Ireland, in 1850 to start a new life.

The young man made his way to Grass Valley, California, to struggle alongside early pioneers in the Golden State, looking for his fortune in the gold fields. Tom's son, Frank E. Sullivan, Sr., was born in 1901, and would spend a lifetime of involvement in the petroleum industry.

For 45 years the elder Frank Sullivan worked in the oil business. Retired since 1966, he now resides in San Francisco. On the day of his father's retirement, Frank Jr. resigned his 18-year position with Standard Oil to begin a new concept in fuel distribution in Kern County.

Frank Jr. met a new challenge in 1966—that of "white collar" distributorship—by allowing the operator of the distributorship to actively pursue new customers

without the burden of driving trucks and delivering fuel as before. His organization, Sullivan Standard Petroleum Company, prospered and was the "first" for Standard Oil's western operations as well as other programs now based on this incentive plan.

The entrepreneur was offered the chance of becoming a "jobber" in 1979, and he commenced the operation where he now buys his own products which he distributes to his customers. The plant fills a large portion of the fuel and lubricant needs of agriculture, commerce, and industry throughout Kern County.

In 1966 Frank Jr. put his roots down in Kern County. Frank Jr. has been married to his wife Diane for more than 30 years. Two of their children now work at Sullivan's Petroleum. Frank Jr. serves as president of the company and his 28-year-old son Timothy is executive vice-president in charge of the day-to-day operations of the concern. Daughter Kerrie works in dispatch processing at the plant and daughter Kolleen attends Bakersfield College. Daughter Kathleen, a graduate of Cal-Poly, is now married and resides in Santa Barbara. The birth of Timothy's son, Francis Evans Sullivan, recently added to the growth of the Sullivan clan.

Frank Sullivan, Jr., looks to the

future. The ultimate in automated fuel dispensing was begun in 1982, when the family began a cardlock operation in downtown Bakersfield on Eye Street between 23rd and 24th streets. They plan to establish three more stations in the near future.

Frank Jr. recently purchased a cattle ranch near Porterville, which he named Sullivan's Shamrock Ranch. It's a cow-calf operation where he will run purebred Beefmaster cattle. Frank Jr. can devote time to this endeavor as Timothy manages the petroleum business.

The Sullivans have come a long way from South County Cork, Ireland. The family has devoted much time and energy to the Bakersfield community. Diane is active with both the Mercy Hospital Auxiliary and the Bakersfield Symphony Orchestra. Frank Jr.'s affiliations include the Petroleum Club and the Elk's Lodge, and he strongly supports the Pyles Boys' Camp, which is sponsored by the oil industry.

Sullivan's Standard Petroleum Company, an example of perseverance and hard work within the American system of free enterprise, is proud to be a part of Bakersfield and Kern County.

Frank Sullivan, Sr., is shown here in 1921 on the site of today's Bank of America Tower in San Francisco.

Frank Sullivan, Jr. (seated), president, with his son Timothy, executive vice-president of Sullivan's Standard Petroleum Company.

EUGENE F. CASSADY & CO.

On August 1, 1955, Eugene Cassady returned to his hometown of Bakersfield to establish an accounting practice. He had been away to serve in the Navy during World War II and the Korean War, obtain a college education, and acquire experience with an international accounting firm.

The Cassadys have been prominent members of the Kern County community since 1887, when Eugene Cassady's grandfather first settled there. His father was a well-known merchant and civic leader.

The firm of Eugene F. Cassady & Co. operated with a low budget and shared offices in its early years, but Cassady soon gained the respect of the community and was able to add members to his staff who shared his desire to build a quality practice that provided a full range of accounting services to Kern County. Many of the current members of the company have been together more than ten years. This longevity has

contributed to an atmosphere in which staff and partners work as a team to serve the diversified needs of their clients.

During the early '60s, Cassady foresaw a period of widespread growth in the accounting profession. In order to accommodate this growth, the firm was one of the first CPA practices in Bakersfield to operate its own electronic data-processing system. Since then, the system has been updated three times to take advantage of improved technology.

While growth has always been important to Eugene F. Cassady & Co., it has been controlled to ensure quality for existing as well as future clients. Since 1955 the concern has moved its office site three times to accommodate its growing staff, and is currently located at 5665 California Avenue, Suite 200, in the heart of the Stockdale business community.

Eugene F. Cassady & Co. has increased the number of its partners to five. Donna Kisela became a

The staff members of Eugene F. Cassady & Co. are (seated, left to right) Donald Hardaway, Jr., partner; Virtys Salter; Maret Johnson; Eugene F. Cassady, partner; and Donna Kisela, partner. Standing (left to right) are Frances Knight; Fred Stine; Rita Miller; Michele Martin; Donald Blankenship, partner; Judith Faulstick, partner; and Al Warnick.

partner in 1972, taking on the responsibility of the firm's administration. Her family, also, has been in the Golden Empire for three generations. Donald Hardaway, Jr., became a partner in 1979, and Judith Faulstick and Donald Blankenship were promoted to partner status in 1983.

Since its inception, Eugene F. Cassady & Co. has striven for excellence in all professional areas, including accounting, taxes, estate planning, management consulting, and private and governmental auditing. Among its service area specializations are petroleum, agriculture, health care, restaurants, and construction.

BAKERSFIELD READY MIX, INC.

Summer, 1954, at the new Olive Drive plant.

While driving along Highway 58, or while observing the cross-valley canal, or while visiting Kern County's southernmost area, Frazier Park, one is never really aware of the construction that made it all possible.

Bakersfield Ready Mix has provided construction materials for a good part of what has developed in the area. The firm supplied the concrete for the Highway 58 bridges and constructed bridges in the freeway portion of the Kern Canyon; completed a great deal of construction in Frazier Park (Bakersfield Ready Mix has a plant in the area); and built the 12-story all-concrete Plaza (Christian) Towers. The all-concrete Cal Almond processing plant and Bakersfield's newest landmark, the 12-story Stockdale Towers on California Avenue, also were served by the company.

Incidentally, in the construction of Tenneco West's almond plant, the largest concrete panels ever created in the Bakersfield area were used. Each tilt slab was 64 feet high and 24 feet wide, with a thickness of one foot. The placement of each 64-ton panel required two 90-ton cranes.

Bakersfield Ready Mix, a family business, was founded in 1954. It was owned and operated by Martin Erreca and Rayburn Dezember. The original equipment consisted of four 6-yard ready-mix trucks and a total of six employees, including an office staff of one.

Martin Erreca passed away on June 24, 1966. Dezember also serves as president and chief executive officer of the American National Bank. He oversees 28 branches in seven counties with assets of almost $600 million and more than 500 employees.

Bakersfield Ready Mix began at Olive Drive near Freeway 99, and moved in 1975 to its present main location on Panama Lane. The firm houses a fleet of 23 trucks serviced by an automated control batch plant that premixes the concrete and automatically weighs the rock, sand, cement, water, and any admixture.

A Ross Jr. Satellite and Uniplant was purchased in 1968; it was used in building approximately 14 miles of the Los Angeles Aqueduct from

The San Emidio Rock Plant, circa 1930, is located near Highway 166 and Old River Road. The plant manufactured rock, sand, and gravel for various Bakersfield Ready Mix construction projects. The plant has been completely rebuilt and has the capacity to manufacture top-quality products. Courtesy of Cal Williams.

Indian Wells to Little Lake, the Chatsworth Canal in Los Angeles, and other operations from its Bakersfield headquarters.

Acquisitions include the Ridgecrest Concrete Company, the Concrete Sales Ready Mix Company on Mt. Vernon, and the long-established Hartman Concrete Company, including a plant in Taft. Especially significant was the purchase in 1972 of Hartman's rock and sand quarry and the crushing plant at San Emidio.

The current officers of Bakersfield Ready Mix, Inc., are Rayburn Dezember, chairman; Ron Davis, president and general manager; and Jack Williams, vice-president in charge of sales.

LLOYD E. PLANK, REALTOR

In our chapter introduction, we wrote of a simple group of early Indians. These early inhabitants had a strict code of justice, a straight-forward approach to life and customs, an unfaltering belief in family and community, and an unwavering desire to perform as well as possible. With these virtues of keeping all traditions and personal beliefs as true as the arrow's flight, they were to be admired.

There is no Indian blood in the Lloyd Plank family, but certain aspects of those early settlers and those who followed have left an unmistakable influence on this local businessman.

There was certainly not much romance in providing the necessary work clothes for the men of the Bakersfield area, but Lloyd held a job at Brock's Department Store back in 1953. Malcolm Brock saw the youthful Plank as a go-getter and swiftly promoted him to shoe buyer for the store.

Moving from Brock's, Plank went on to men's clothing and was subsequently named manager of Coffee's. It was during this period that Lloyd developed a strong friendship with Jack Bailey, who was manager of Karpe Real Estate.

Encouraged by Bailey in 1971 to enter the exciting world of providing "just the right home" for local families, Lloyd repaid that friendship by distinguishing himself as the firm's Salesman of the Year for three consecutive years: 1972, 1973, 1974.

He opened his own three-person office in 1975, and during that same year the Bakersfield Board of Realtors named him Salesman of the Year. (Three other members of the Plank company have since received the same honor.) In 1982 the Board of Realtors named Lloyd Broker of the Year.

With annual sales of $70 million, the Stockdale-based organization features several divisions. Among their activities are the marketing of new-home and condominium construction (Plank has built several hundred new homes over the past few years) and the relocation of individuals and families on a nationwide basis, closely coordinating with scores of local firms. Plank also has a probate division; it is one of the few Bakersfield businesses specializing in this highly complex area of real estate. Lloyd Plank is his firm's certified real estate appraiser.

Guidance, support, and assistance have been provided by Lloyd's wife Patty and son Russell "Rusty." Lloyd is actively involved with St. Phillip's Catholic Church, is past chairman of the Cancer Crusade, has spent two terms as chairman of the Convention and Visitors Bureau of the Greater Bakersfield Chamber of Commerce, is a life director and past president of the Better Business Bureau and the Downtown Business Association, and, in 1983, was named Bakersfield's Rotarian of the year.

Two important recent mergers have strengthened Plank's sales force with experienced local real estate people. Goldie's Gallery of Homes and the Ferris Company joined the Plank organization in 1981 and 1982, respectively.

There are currently 25 members of the sales staff, including 15 brokers and five support people. All are trained and educated in the real estate business; eight are graduates of the Real Estate Institute.

Lloyd Plank and his philosophy can be described by a much-used Indian expression—"straight arrow." That arrow continues to point to success and achievement for Lloyd E. Plank, Realtor.

TEJON RANCH COMPANY

Tejon Ranch is bigger than the combined areas of Chicago, Philadelphia, Boston, and San Francisco; is three-eighths the size of Rhode Island; and could encompass the city of Los Angeles within its boundaries.

The first inhabitants of the ranchos that comprise the Tejon Ranch Company were three main tribes of Indians: the Yokuts who resided on the northern portions of the ranch from the floor of the San Joaquin Valley to the Tehachapi Pass; the Kitanemuk who lived in the area of the old ranch headquarters on Tejon Creek, which was later to become the Sebastian Indian Reserve; and the Chumash who traversed Grapevine Canyon, establishing winter quarters at the mouth of the canyon, with summer camp at Castec Lake. The Aliklik from the southern areas also had a village site at Castec Lake.

The following brief chronological diary allows the presentation of historical highlights—each event could fill a volume by itself:

1772 — Captain Don Pedro Fagés, a Spanish soldier, was the first white man to travel north through the Tejon (via Grapevine Canyon) to Buena Vista Lake.

1776 — Padre Francisco Garcés was the first white man to enter the Tejon Old Headquarters area via Tejon Creek.

1806 — Lt. Francisco Ruiz originated the name "Tejon" (badger) when his soldiers found a dead badger at the mouth of the canyon to which he gave the name. He also named Cañada de las Uvas (Grapevine Canyon) because of the abundance of cimarron grape vines.

1827 — Jedediah Strong Smith started the flow of trappers, traders, and explorers into the Tehachapi Mountain area. He was followed by such men as Kit Carson and Ewing Young in 1830.

1837 — Peter LeBeck (Lebeque or Lebec), a French trapper, was killed by a bear on October 17 at the site of what was later to become Fort Tejon.

1843 — Mexican land grants included Rancho Los Alamos Y Agua Caliente, Rancho El Tejon, and Rancho de Castec.

1844 — John C. Frémont, Kit Carson, and Alex Godey traveled south over Tejon Creek Pass and

---

Fort Tejon, looking from east to west across the parade grounds divided by Grapevine Creek, circa 1890.

John Oak Creek Pass. Frémont mistook this pass for Walker's Pass.

1846 — Mexican-American War — Edward Fitzgerald Beale, his Delaware Indian servant, and Kit Carson went for reinforcements during the battle of San Pascuál.

1848 — Beale, as Navy lieutenant, carried the first news of gold to Washington, beating the Army (Kit Carson) by two months.

1853 — Sebastian (Reserve) Indian Reservation was established. Containing 75,000 acres (surveyed by H.D. Washburn), it was named after Senator William King Sebastian of Arkansas and was inhabited by 500 to 2,000 Indians.

1853 — Lieutenant R.S. Williamson traveled the Tejon Pass with a railroad survey party.

1853 — Joaquín Murrieta, called the "Robin Hood of California," had a silver and copper mine (so the story goes) in the Tehachapi Mountains which he worked with imported slave labor. Murrieta's head and Three-fingered Jack's hand were brought to Beale and then taken to San Francisco for display. (This later was reported not to be the head of Murrieta by those who knew him.)

1853 — First sheep raising on the Tejon Ranch, for the Sebastian Indian Reserve, was on Rancho La Liebre.

1854 — Beale's Indians built the first canal in the valley to irrigate wheat on the reservation.

1854 — Fort Tejon was established by First Brigoons on August 10 (recommended by Edward Beale),

Rose's Station, viewed here in the 1890s, was a trading post, water stop for stages, and the center of social activity for the area.

with an average of 225 troops. Twenty-five structures were built at a cost of more than $.5 million.

1855 —Rancho La Liebre was deeded to Mary Edward Beale from William C. Walker on August 8. The 48,799 acres sold for $1,500.

1857 —Rose's Station, or Rancho Canoa, became a trading post and water stop for stages and was also the center of social activities for the Tejon area.

1857—A great earthquake occurred at Fort Tejon on January 19.

1858 —U.S. Camel Corps was established at Fort Tejon. Delivered by Beale and Arab camelmen, the camels were used until 1861.

1858 —Butterfield Overland Stage line established two stations on the Tejon, one at Fort Tejon and the other at Comanche Point.

1860 —First telegraph service from Los Angeles to San Francisco passed through Fort Tejon.

This 1890s dairy ranch was north of what is now Lebec.

Some of the early Indians who inhabited the Tejon Cañon, which is part of the Tejon Ranch Company today.

1868 —"Cross and Crescent" brand recorded in Kern County as a cattle brand. Sometimes referred to as "Tejon's Mission Bell" brand, it was actually the "Cross and Crescent" brand that appeared on cattle imported from Spain and purchased for the Sebastian Indian Reserve. It originated about the year 1212 in Spain and is a combination of the Christian Cross and Arabian Crescent, and was created when an Arab married into a Spanish family.

1879 —Beale's sheep drive (with 16,000 head) from Cow Springs (Antelope Valley) to Green River, Wyoming, herded by his flockmaster, José Jesús López, arrived with approximately 11,000 head plus 3,000 head purchased by Lopez in Red Bluff.

1880 —Beale returned to California and started raising cattle.

1886 —A Swiss party began a cheese factory near Lebec without much success. (The cows were too difficult to catch in the mountains.)

1893 —General Beale died, leaving his property to his son and heir, Truxtun Beale.

1900 —Beale Memorial Library, the first free library for children in Kern County, was erected.

1904 —Beale Clock Tower was built at the intersection of Chester and 17th streets. It now resides at the Kern County Museum.

1908 —Los Angeles Aqueduct construction began to bring water from Bishop through Rancho La Liebre to Los Angeles.

1912 —Chandler and Sherman, along with 30 businessmen, purchased Tejon Ranchos.

1915 —Mrs. Anna B. Knowles started a career that lasted more than 35 years as the only teacher of the Tejon Indian Elementary School. (Mrs. Knowles was the aunt of this publication's co-author—the late Richard C. Bailey.)

1936 —Tejon Ranch Company was incorporated on February 14, with 108,000 shares of stock outstanding.

1973 —Tejon Ranch stock began trading on the American Stock Exchange.

Today the Tejon Ranch, encompassing almost 270,000 acres, is a multifaceted organization involved in livestock, oil and minerals, commercial land uses, game management, farming, and crop research.

Tejon is the largest contiguous private land holding in the state of California and one of the nation's great ranches. It is a vital part of our history.

ICARDO FARMS

There was not an abundance of vegetables and produce in the southern San Joaquin Valley in the 1940s. In the Mettler area, alfalfa, grains, and cotton were the only basic crops at that time.

Jimmie Icardo helped turn the arid land into fertile productivity when he and his brother Enrico started farming the area in 1947. Two years later Jimmie Icardo formed his own company, to be known as Jimmie Icardo Farms.

The Icardo family emigrated from Northern Italy to the Tehachapi area in 1908. The senior Icardo later moved to the San Fernando Valley and started vegetable farming in Sepulveda. Jimmie and his brothers worked the farms during the summers, on weekends, and during vacations. (Jimmie recalls attending school in Van Nuys with Jane Russell and Bob Waterfield.)

Following the move to Mettler, Jimmie, his wife Marjorie, and their three children took advantage of the sale of used government surplus property at Garner Field near Taft. They converted a warehouse into a packing shed, another into apartments for field workers, and refurbished an Air Corps utility building into a residence for the family. This was their home until the family moved to Bakersfield.

In the early 1950s a farmer friend, Victor Machado, asked Icardo and several neighbors to help establish a bank on his Greenfield property. That was the beginning of the Greenfield State Bank, which now has offices in Bakersfield, Lancaster, and Quartz Hills. Presently, Jimmie Icardo is the only active member of the original group and serves as chairman of the board of the renamed California Republic Bank.

Jimmie has always been active in community functions. He helped start the Mettler Farm Bureau and Progressive Club. He, and friends and

Jimmie Icardo and his son Gary, circa 1960.

neighbors, used leftover materials from the Taft St. Christopher's Church to build a small church in Mettler. With other friends and neighbors, the creative Jimmie established the Ridge Ginning Company, Kern Ridge Growers Inc., and San Joaquin Capital Inc. (now involved in developing the Sheraton Hotel adjacent to the Civic Auditorium).

Besides Enrico, Jimmie has three other brothers. Albert and Arthur farm in the Mettler area; Jack owns and operates the Mettler Farm House Cafe on Highway 99; a sister, Mrs. Albena Jones, lives in San Diego; Jimmie's daughters, Gloria Collins and Yvonne Gonzales, both live in Bakersfield. Jimmie's mother, now 100 years of age, resides in a Bakersfield rest home.

During the past five years Jimmie's son Gary has been overseeing the farming operations, leaving Jimmie more free time to devote to his civic interests and other investments.

"It's all been good to me, thanks to my family, friends, and neighbors," says Jimmie. And Jimmie Icardo has been good to Bakersfield and Kern County.

Jimmie Icardo's favorite tractor, now retired.

CHEVRON USA, INC.

Above
This 1900s mule-drawn tanker is in marked contrast to Chevron's 18-wheel tankers on the highway today.

Top
Thousands of wood derricks dotted the 11C field headquarters in Taft.

Chevron USA, Inc., a subsidiary of Standard Oil Company of California, is responsible for domestic operations while the parent corporation handles international operations.

The firm got its start in the 1870s when Frederick Taylor first struck oil in the Pico Canyon area north of Los Angeles. The venture was known as Taylor's California Star Oil Works.

On September 10, 1879, Taylor, along with some oil merchants and investors, incorporated in San Francisco to form the Pacific Coast Oil Company.

The company prospered and expanded operations but was finally unable to meet the fierce competition in this new industry. Pacific Coast Oil might have gone bankrupt or dissolved before the turn of the century if a financial benefactor had not arrived to support the company and provide guidance.

John D. Rockefeller and his partners, owners of the Standard Oil organization, as part of their continuing effort to expand, purchased Pacific Coast Oil in 1900 and allowed it to continue in Bakersfield, Kern County, and other Southern California locations under its own name.

In 1902-1903 Pacific Coal Oil had constructed the first major pipeline in California extending from the Kern River Field in Bakersfield to the Richmond Refinery, approximately 250 miles north.

In 1906 the Pacific Oil Company changed its name to Standard Oil, eventually becoming Standard Oil Company of California following the breakup of Rockefeller's Standard Oil in 1911.

Standard Oil drilled its first exploratory well in 1910 in the Midway Field near Taft. It has been credited with being the first successful drilling with rotary tools in California.

Standard Oil Company of California reorganized to create Chevron USA, Inc., in 1977.

Currently Chevron USA, in operations directed from Bakersfield, produces over 90,000 barrels per day of crude, including oil from operations at Elk Hills Naval Petroleum Reserve, and supervises 1,900 miles of pipelines that transport about 240,000 barrels per day in Central and Northern California.

All of these pipelines, including a product line that delivers gasoline from their Richmond Refinery to Sacramento, Banta, and San Jose, operate from an office in Bakersfield. Chevron continues to operate a 26,000-barrel-per-day refinery in Bakersfield, producing gasoline and diesel fuel for the San Joaquin Valley.

The Chevron Land and Development Company is also very active today, overseeing residential and industrial properties.

With approximately 850 local employees and 100 to 150 individual contracting firms, Chevron USA continues to help shape the future, a future that started over 100 years ago in Bakersfield.

GULF OIL CORPORATION

Spindletop, one of the most famous oil wells in the world, blew in on January 10, 1901, establishing Texas as a major oil source. A few months later the Gulf Refining Company ("Gulf" referred to the Gulf of Mexico) was chartered. It was the beginning of what would become the Gulf Oil Corporation.

Events that followed included the discovery of oil in 1905 at Glenn Pool near Tulsa, Oklahoma; over-water drilling for oil in 1910 in Louisiana; and the first drive-in service station in 1913, in Pittsburgh, Pennsylvania. In 1914 the first foreign production operation in Mexico was started; it was followed by a 1924 Venezuela endeavor. In 1934 the Kuwait Oil Company was established, with Gulf owning a 50-percent interest.

W.L. Mellon retired as chairman of the board in 1948 after 46 years of service. Later years of diversification, multiple transactions, marketing, new discoveries, restructuring, and joint ventures have made Gulf Oil a leader in the continuing search for new energy sources.

A special luncheon for 43 retired Bakersfield Gulf employees was held at the Gulf Oil headquarters building on Stockdale Highway in April 1983. The retirees were previously informed that the purpose of the meeting was twofold: an opportunity to meet and reminisce with fellow retirees, and an opportunity to assist in the writing of this story. The get-together was hosted by J.L. Goolsby, area production manager, and Frank Mize, manager of environmental and safety. The early days and history of Gulf in Bakersfield and Kern County were pleasantly relived.

Gulf Oil old-timer O. Lee Wix was present and recalled his days as a topographer for the Pacific Eastern Production Company. Mr. Wix established the first Gulf Oil office in Bakersfield in 1926 at 1929 Maple Street. The first well was drilled (KCL-B No. 1) in the Fruitvale area in 1928. (That same well is still pumping today.) An office and warehouse were built in the Fruitvale Field in 1931.

The Paloma Field, 18 miles southwest of Bakersfield in the Buena Vista Lake bottom, was discovered in 1939; and in 1943 six companies joined in developing it with Gulf Oil as the operator.

The Bakersfield office became the hub for other developments and acquisitions such as the Oak Canyon

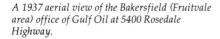

An attendant poses with an earlier-vintage gas pump of Gulf Oil. The firm's first Bakersfield offices were opened in 1926.

Field in 1941, located near Castaic, next to today's Magic Mountain. Developments in California known as Yorba Linda, Tejon, Ventura, Arvin, Edison, and Woodward, in the Midway-Sunset field, were also under the Bakersfield office.

In 1960 Gulf Oil Company of California purchased Universal Consolidated Oil Company, through which it acquired additional properties and many more oil fields in the Bakersfield area.

Gulf Oil offices were consolidated in Bakersfield in 1965 and the firm continued production and exploration activities in the western states and Alaska.

The history of Gulf Oil's Bakersfield operations came alive again in the reminiscences of the retired employees—those who had contributed to the development of Gulf Oil in the Golden Empire.

A 1937 aerial view of the Bakersfield (Fruitvale area) office of Gulf Oil at 5400 Rosedale Highway.

BAKERSFIELD COLLEGE

In 1913, 20 students of the Kern County Union High School District enrolled in a "fifth year" of secondary school courses. The only campus of the University of California was at Berkeley—far from home—and these students were preparing to transfer there after a year or two of college-level instruction from their high school teachers. From these modest beginnings, supervised by assistant principal Paul Vandereike, has grown a community college with over 11,000 students and 225 full-time professors, recognized as one of the finest in the nation.

In 1917 Grace Van Dyke Bird was hired to teach some high school courses and college-level French. Later she assumed counseling and administrative duties, becoming dean of the junior college in 1920, the only woman among all the deans of junior colleges in California.

When the student body grew to 900 and the faculty to 65, Bakersfield Junior College moved in 1935 into a separate building, Warren Hall, across the street from the high school.

Grace Bird guided the college through the staff shortages and enrollment declines (to 200 students) of the World War II years. In 1946 veterans returned, enrollments climbed to 450, and Grace Bird was named director. She resigned in 1950 after 32 years of service. She was succeeded by Ralph Prator, the first administrator to be given the title of president, who changed the name of the institution to Bakersfield College. Ed Simonsen, who followed Prator as president, later became chancellor of the Kern Community College District. Other presidents have been

A 1955 view from the top of Memorial Stadium showing the construction of the men's and women's physical education and health centers.

Burns Finlinson, John Collins, and (currently) Richard Wright.

The present 153-acre site at 1801 Panorama Drive was first occupied in 1956, housing a student body of 1,400 and a faculty of 89. Residence halls were named for emeriti Ralph Prator, former president, and Margaret Levinson, former dean of instruction. In 1960 voters approved a separate college district. By 1964 the Kern Community College District had been joined by five bordering high school districts. Porterville College was annexed in 1967 and Cerro Coso College, Ridgecrest, was opened in 1973.

In 1975 the district purchased, at a bargain price, a former department store building at 21st and Chester streets. It was remodeled to accommodate the district offices and the Downtown Center, an outreach center of Bakersfield College specializing in open-entry courses. Another outreach center has been maintained in Delano since 1972, offering afternoon and evening courses for the convenience of residents in Delano, Shafter, and McFarland.

Bakersfield College now offers 99 programs leading to the degrees of associate in arts and associate in science. Students may complete all general education requirements for bachelors' degrees at this convenient, low-cost, high-quality college and transfer up to 70 units to four-year colleges and universities. Certificates of achievement are offered in 39 vocational-technical areas. The college also offers community service classes and special-interest workshops at nominal cost. Cultural events such as concerts, plays, lectures, and sporting events also are sponsored by the college at little or no cost to the audience.

Bakersfield College, 1983.

149

BORTON, PETRINI & CONRON

Two men of singular personalities and styles guided the growth of a law firm formed in Bakersfield in 1923, which in the succeeding 60 years became one of the most successful in Central California and the largest between Sacramento and Los Angeles.

Fred E. Borton was a classic gentleman: elegant, gracious, and conservative. A complementary personality, James Petrini was flamboyant and ambitious. This heterogenous alliance lent itself well toward nurturing a developing enterprise, and in 1933 the scholarly and industrious personality of Harry C. Conron was added as the third ingredient of the composite. Many people believe that the unique combination of their compatible personalities has provided the key to the success of the firm known as Borton, Petrini & Conron, which now numbers over 30 attorneys.

While the modern organization dated from the partnership of Borton and Petrini in 1923, its origins go back to 1899 when Borton (after being graduated from the University of California, Hastings College of Law) came to Bakersfield as a law clerk for Kern County Superior Court Judge John Bennette. Three years later the young man opened his own practice in the old Bank of Italy building at 19th and H streets.

A large number of the operations that pioneered and developed Kern County were served by Borton, Petrini & Conron—including Southern Pacific Company, Santa Fe, Kern County Land Company, and Standard Oil Corporation. A knowledgeable leader in laws pertaining to oil and gas, real estate, water, and transportation, the early enterprise handled many of the most

colorful civil cases in the San Joaquin Valley.

The three partners, while busy establishing a thriving law firm, still found time for bar activities; and all were members of the board of governors of the California State Bar Association. As a result of discerning recruitments, the organization has a rich history of past members and partners.

In 1938 Fred Borton's son Richard joined the group, specializing in personal-injury cases. After 25 years of practice he was elevated in 1964 to the Kern County Superior Court, where he presided until his retirement in 1981.

George A. Brown became an associate in 1948 and was made a partner four years later, a relationship he maintained until his appointment to the Superior Court bench in 1969. Judge Brown established himself during his 20 years with Borton, Petrini, & Conron as a dedicated, articulate, and learned attorney. His extraordinary combination of trial skill and analytical ability led to his appointment to the Fifth District Court of Appeal in 1971 and his appointment as chief justice in 1972—a position he still holds.

Walter H. Condley held a partnership in the firm from 1952 until 1966, at which time he was named a municipal court judge. His keen legal vision and no-nonsense approach to the law has served the community well, and resulted in his elevation to the Kern County Superior Court.

The practice of Borton, Petrini & Conron has expanded in scope, number, and territory. Comprised of more than 30 attorneys, the organization has branch offices in Santa Maria, San Luis Obispo,

Visalia, Santa Barbara, Sacramento, and Fresno. Utilizing a strong foundation of professional minds and methods to enable it to better assist an active statewide clientele, the firm has extended its services and provides lawyers emphasizing practices in real property, probate, estate planning, water, oil and gas, public entity, labor, tax, personal injury, patent, and corporate, as well as general business.

Borton, Petrini & Conron occupies the entire top floor of the new Westchester Corporate Plaza. Although Kern County's oldest law firm, it looks forward to the future and has invested in the most modern computer, word-processing, and telecommunications equipment available to the legal community.

The addition of two respected attorneys in "of counsel" positions is indicative that the organization knows the value of experience. Roy Gargano, who joined the group in 1978, had served as county counsel of Kern County from 1951 to 1963, when he was appointed to the Kern County Superior Court. In 1966 he was promoted to the position of associate justice of the California Court of Appeal, Fifth Appellate District—a position he held until his retirement in 1977. Albert M. Leddy became associated in 1983, ending 13 years of service as district attorney of Kern County. Prior to that appointment he had been engaged in private practice in Kern County since 1950.

The legal profession and the Bakersfield community have certainly been well represented by Borton, Petrini & Conron as the firm continues in its time-honored tradition of service assisting those in need of legal advice.

Fred E. Borton

James Petrini

Harry C. Conron

George A. Brown

Richard Borton

Walter H. Condley

PATRONS

The following individuals, companies, and organizations have made a valuable commitment to the quality of this publication. Windsor Publications and the Greater Bakersfield Chamber of Commerce gratefully acknowledge their participation in *Heart of the Golden Empire: An Illustrated History of Bakersfield.*

Advance Beverage Co., Inc.
Atlantic Richfield Company
BA-Valley Industrial Supply
Bakersfield Californian*
Bakersfield City School District
Bakersfield College*
Bakersfield Ready Mix, Inc.*
Bakersfield Sandstone Brick Company*
Dr. and Mrs. William D. Bezdek
Blackwell Land Company, Inc.
Borton, Petrini & Conron*
Christopher D. Brewer's Historical Consultants
Brindle Boiler Works, Inc.
Brock's Department Store*
Calcot, Ltd.*
Curt Carter
Eugene F. Cassady & Co.*
Chevron USA, Inc.*
Fred and Renee Cummings
J.L. Denio, Inc.*
Mel Denio
First American Title Insurance Company
Floyd's Stores, Inc.*
Fox & Company CPAs
Goodwill Industries of Kern County
Gulf Oil Corporation*
Eleanor Lindsay Hample
Home Savings of America
Leo C. and Karol A. Hudson, Jr.
H&R Block
Icardo Farms*
Johnston Farms
Judds Specialty Shop
Kern County Heritage Commission

Kern High School District
Kern Radiology and Nuclear Medical Group, Inc.
KERO-TV23*
KGET-Kern Golden Empire Television
Lambourne Travel Service, Inc.
Lufkin's Business College*
Mercy Hospital*
Mossman Enterprises, Inc.
Mr. and Mrs. Philip H. Niederauer
Occidental Exploration and Production Company*
Lloyd E. Plank, Realtor*
Price Waterhouse
Reliable Moving, Inc.
Rio Bravo Resort*
Russell & Owens Engineering & Surveying
San Joaquin Community Hospital*
Security Pacific National Bank Business Banking Center
Sheats, Willman, Woken, Mihal & Hooper, CPAs
Shell California Production Inc.*
South Union Truck Repair, Inc.
Mr. and Mrs. Don Stewart
Stewart Title
Sullivan's Standard Petroleum Company*
Tejon Ranch Company*
Tenneco West*
Congressman Bill Thomas
Mr. and Mrs. John N. Thompson
Wally Tucker Datsun*
Turner Crane Service, Incorporated
United News Co.
Urner's
Wickersham Jewelers*
June Wilson
Stroud Wilson

*Partners in Progress of *Heart of the Golden Empire: An Illustrated History of Bakersfield.* The histories of these companies and organizations appear in Chapter 8, beginning on page 121.

ABOUT THE AUTHOR

"Bakersfield, the heart of Kern County, has an essence like no other city. To some it is the vestigial vibration of the Old Frontier and Manifest Destiny; to others, the breath of the Promised Land, a realm of hope and progress."

—*Richard Clayton Bailey, 1982*

Richard Clayton Bailey—author, teacher, historian—is known throughout Kern County for a lifetime of achievement. Richard Bailey spent over 50 years of his life studying and sharing the history of Bakersfield, Kern County, and Central California; and, through speaking, teaching, and writing, he brought that history to life for thousands of Californians.

Richard Bailey arrived in Bakersfield in 1929 as a very young man. To Richard, Bakersfield was a magical slice of the Old West he had read so much about. With an enthusiasm he never lost, he explored Bakersfield and Kern County. Making friends with the old-timers and Indians, he collected their stories and distilled their memories into a rich body of historical knowledge.

After graduating from Bakersfield Community College and from the Petroleum Technology School in Coalinga, he earned a degree in education and history from Fresno State University, and taught on all levels. Because he believed so deeply that local history was the ideal tool to make learning relevant, he was asked to join the staff of the new Kern County Museum. Richard remained at the museum for 32 years, serving as its director for 26 years.

Among his achievements was the development of Pioneer Village, which depicts the lives of pioneers in the southern San Joaquin Valley between 1868 and 1910. The village is widely recognized as the "Williamsburg of the West," and is the largest and most authentic development of its kind on the Pacific Coast. The Petroleum Museum, one of the outstanding historic oil exhibits in the United States, is another significant addition to the Kern County Museum complex that was developed under Richard Bailey's direction. He also initiated the Lori Brock Junior Museum, a hands-on institution that serves the children of the community.

Throughout his long career Richard conducted tours through Central California, and he became a recognized expert in taping local history interviews and in preserving local history. He was instrumental in the placement of many historical plaques and successfully encouraged the formation of small museums in almost every town in Kern County. The author of numerous books, magazine and newspaper articles, Richard Bailey's published works include *Collector's Choice, Heritage of Kern, Explorations of Kern, Kern County Place Names,* and *Chronology of Kern.* He is listed in *Who's Who in the West* and *Who's Who in America.*

In addition to his professional achievements, Richard Bailey enriched the lives of countless Kern County residents by sharing his friendship, his boundless enthusiasm, and his love for the region in which he chose to live. *Heart of the Golden Empire* is Richard Bailey's last published work. It will stand as a fitting tribute to this outstanding citizen of Kern, who will long be remembered for his lasting contributions to Bakersfield and Kern County.

Richard Clayton Bailey (1911-1983)

SELECTED BIBLIOGRAPHY

Angell, Myron. *History of the Counties of Fresno, Tulare, Kern.* 1892. Reprint. Chicago: The Lewis Publishing Co., 1974.

Bailey, Richard C. *Chronology of Kern County.* Bakersfield, CA: The Kern County Museum, 1979.

_____. *Explorations In Kern.* Bakersfield, CA: Kern County Historical Society, 1974.

_____. *Heritage of Kern.* Bakersfield, CA: Kern County Historical Society, 1974.

Bain, Naomi E. *The Story of Colonel Thomas Baker and the Founding of Bakersfield.* Bakersfield, CA: Kern County Historical Society, 1942.

Baker, John. *San Joaquin Vignettes.* Bakersfield, CA: Kern County Historical Society, 1955.

Baker, Thomas A. *Early Bakersfield.* Bakersfield, CA: Kern County Historical Society, 1937.

Bancroft, Hubert Howe. *History of California.* Vols. 1, 3, 4, 6, 7. San Francisco: The History Company, 1890.

Bann, Robert T. *The Shafter Pioneers.* Typed copy, February 24, 1961.

Beattie, George William. *California's Unbuilt Missions, Spanish Plans for an Inland Chain.* East Highlands, CA: George William Beattie, 1930.

Berg, Norman. *A History of Kern County Land Company.* Bakersfield, CA: Kern County Historical Society, 1971.

Bishop, William Henry. "Southern California, Part 2." *Harper's Bazaar* 1882. Reprint. *Southern California, 100 Years Ago.* Albuquerque: Sun Publishing Company, 1976.

Blodget, Rush Maxwell. *Little Dramas of Old Bakersfield.* Los Angeles: Carl A. Bundy Quill & Press, 1931.

Bolton, Herbert Eugene. *In the South San Joaquin Ahead of Garces.* Bakersfield, CA: Kern County Historical Society, 1935.

Bonsal, Stephen. *Edward Fitzgerald Beale: A Pioneer in the Path of Empire, 1822-1903.* New York: G.P.

Putnam's Sons, 1912.

Boyd, William Harland. *A California Middle Border.* Richardson, Texas: The Havilah Press, 1972.

_____. Ludeke, John, and Rump, Marjorie, eds. *Inside Historic Kern.* Bakersfield, CA: Kern County Historic Society, 1982.

_____. *Stagecoach Hayday in the San Joaquin Valley.* Bakersfield, CA: Kern County Historical Society, 1983.

Brock, John, Jr. *An Illustrated History of Kern County.* Bakersfield, CA: Kern County Historical Society, 1976.

Burmeister, Eugene. *City Along The Kern.* Bakersfield, CA: Kern Publishing House, 1969.

Cleland, Robert Glass. *The Cattle on a Thousand Hills.* San Marino, CA: The Huntington Library, 1951.

Cooper, Margaret Aseman. *Land, Water, and Settlement in Kern County, California: 1850-1890.* Berkeley, CA: University of California, 1954. Mimeographed.

Crites, Arthur S. *Pioneer Days in Kern County.* Los Angeles: The Ward Ritchie Press, 1951.

Crofutt, George A. *Crofutt's New Overland Tourist, and Pacific Coast Guide.* Omaha, Nebraska: The Overland Publishing Co., 1880.

Cullimore, Clarence. *The Martyrdom and Interment of Padre Francisco Garces.* Bakersfield, CA: Kern County Historical Society, 1954.

Derby, George H. *The Topographical Reports of Lieutenant George H. Derby.* San Francisco: California Historical Society, 1933.

Doctor, Joseph E. *Shotguns On Sunday.* Los Angeles: Westernlore Press, 1958.

Egan, Feral. *Fremont, Explorer for a Restless Nation.* Garden City, New York: Doubleday & Co., 1977.

Elliott, Wallace E. *History of Kern County with Illustrations.* Reprint. Bakersfield, CA: Merchants Printing & Lithographing Co., 1965.

Fredrickson, David A., and Grossman, Joel W. "A San Dieguito Component at Buena Vista Lake, California." *Journal of California Anthropology* 4: no. 2 (1977), 173-190.

Galvin, John. *A Record of Travels in Arizona and California, 1775-1776, Fr. Francisco Garces.* San Francisco: John Howell-Books, 1967.

Gates, Paul W. *Land Policies in Kern County.* Bakersfield, CA: Kern County Historical Society, 1978.

Gifford, Edward W., and Schenck, W. Egbert. *Archeology of the Southern San Joaquin Valley, California.* Berkeley, CA: University of California, 1926.

Harpending, Ausbury. *The Great Diamond Hoax and Other Stirring Incidents in the Life of Ausbury Harpending.* Edited by James H. Wilkins. San Francisco: The James H. Berry Co., 1913.

Harrell, Alfred. "History of Kern County Newspapers." *Kern County Historical Society Annual Publication.* 3 (1937): 3-9.

Harrington, Edmund Ross. *A History of the Office of the Kern County Superintendent of Schools.* Bakersfield, CA: Kern County Historical Society, 1969.

Heffernan, William J. *Edward M. Kern: The Travels of an Artist-Explorer.* Bakersfield, CA: Kern County Historical Society, 1953.

Hine, Robert V. *California's Utopian Colonies.* San Marino, CA: The Huntington Library, 1953.

_____. *Edward Kern and American Expansion.* New Haven, CT: Yale University Press, 1962.

Hittell, Theodore H. *The Adventures of James Capen Adams, Mountaineer and Grizzly Bear Hunter of California.* New York: Charles Scribner's Sons, 1911.

Irving, Washington. *The Adventures of Captain Bonneville, U.S.A., in the Rocky Mountains and the Far West.* New York: George P. Putnam, 1949.

Kip, William I. *The Early Days of My Episcopate.* New York: Thomas Whittaker, 1892.

Klier, Larry, ed. *Behind the Badge.* Bakersfield, CA: Kern County Sheriff's Welfare and Benefit Association, 1965.

Kroeber, A.L. *Handbook of the Indians of California.* 1925. Reprint. New York: Dover Publications, 1976.

Latta, Frank F. *Black Gold in the Joaquin.* Caldwell, Idaho: Caxton Printers, Ltd., 1949.

———. *El Camino Viejo a Los Angeles.* Bakersfield, CA: Kern County Historical Society, 1936.

———. *Handbook of Yokuts Indians.* 1949. 2nd rev. ed. Santa Cruz, CA: Bear State Books, 1977.

Magruder, Genevieve Kratka. *The Upper San Joaquin Valley, 1772-1870.* Bakersfield, CA: Kern County Historical Society, 1950.

Mayfield, T.J. *Uncle Jeff's Story, A Tale of a San Joaquin Valley Pioneer and His Life with the Yokuts Indians.* Edited by F.F. Latta. Tulare, CA: Tulare Times, 1929.

Miller, Thelma B. *History of Kern County, California.* Vols. 1 and 2. Chicago: S.J. Clarke Publishing Co., 1929.

Mitchell, Edward. *History of Research at Sharktooth Hill, Kern County, California.* Bakersfield, CA: Kern County Historical Society, 1965.

Morgan, Wallace M. *History of Kern County, California.* Los Angeles: Historic Record Company, 1914.

Neihardt, John G. *The Splendid Wayfaring, The Exploits and Adventures of Jedediah Smith and the Ashley-Henry Men, 1822-1831.* Lincoln, NE: University of Nebraska Press, 1970.

Nordhoff, Charles. *California: For Health, Pleasure, and Residence.* New York: Harper & Brothers, 1872.

Oakley, Edward W., ed. *Our Tribute.* Bakersfield, CA: Bakersfield Californian, 1947.

Paquette, Mary Grace. *Basques to Bakersfield.* Bakersfield, CA: Kern County Historical Society, 1982.

———. *Lest We Forget, The History of the French in Kern County.* Bakersfield, CA: Kern County Historical Society, 1978.

Pifer, Phil. *The 100 Year History of the Fire Department of Bakersfield, California.* Bakersfield, CA: Bakersfield Firemen's Relief Association, 1976.

Powers, Bob. *Kern River Country.* Pasadena, CA: Westernlore Publications, 1979.

Powers, Stephen. *Tribes of California.* 1877. Reprint. Berkeley, CA: University of California Press, 1976.

Rintoul, William. *Spudding In, Recollections of Pioneer Days in the California Oil Fields.* San Francisco: California Historical Society, 1976.

Rojas, Arnold R. *These Were the Vaqueros, Collected Works of Arnold Rojas.* San Fernando, CA: Able Printing, 1974.

Said, B.K. *The Pioneers, Bakersfield in its Pioneer Days.* Bakersfield, CA: The Society of Kern County Pioneers, 1910.

Signor, John R. *Southern Pacific-Santa Fe Tehachapi.* San Marino, CA: Golden West Books, 1983.

Smith, Wallace. *Garden of the Sun.* 1939. Reprint. Fresno, CA: California State University, Fresno, 1960.

Spindt, Herman A. *Notes on the Life of Edward M. Kern.* Bakersfield, CA: Kern County Historical Society, 1939.

Stockton, Jesse D. *Those Who Serve, 1917-1944.* Bakersfield, CA: Frank S. Reynolds Post No. 26, Department of California, American Legion, 1944.

Thompson, Thomas H. *Official Historical Map of Tulare County, Brief Sketch of the Early History of Tulare County.* 1892. Reprint. Bakersfield, CA: Merchants Printing & Lithographing Co., 1973.

Thornton, Jim; Bruszewski, Chester;

Dyar, Cecil; Graydon, Ken; and Hofman, Harry, eds. *Delano, Land of Promise.* Delano: Delano Historical Society, 1965.

Tracy, Fannie C., and Rodgers, Glendon J. *The Tracy Saga.* Bakersfield, CA: Cardon House, 1962.

Treadwell, Edward F. *The Cattle King.* New York: The Macmillan Co., 1931.

Turner, John. *White Gold Comes to California.* Bakersfield, CA: California Planting Cotton Seed Distributors, 1981.

Voltmer, Barbara Boyd. *Kern County's Courier, 1866-1876.* Bakersfield, CA: Kern County Historical Society, 1968.

Walker, Ardis M. *Sierra Prologue, Recollections of the Kern Frontier.* Bakersfield, CA: Kern County Historical Society, 1938.

Walker, Edwin F. *Excavation of a Yokuts Indian Cemetery.* Bakersfield, CA: Kern County Historical Society, 1947.

Weeks, George F., ed. *Special Railroad Edition, Bakersfield Californian.* Bakersfield, CA: The Californian, 1895.

Williamson, Lieutenant R.S. *Report of Explorations in California for Railroad Routes to Connect with the Routes Near the 35th and 32d Parallels of North Latitude.* Washington, D.C.: Beverley Tucker, Printer, 1856.

Wilson, Neill C., and Taylor, Frank J. *Southern Pacific, The Roaring Story of a Fighting Railroad.* New York: McGraw-Hill Book Co., 1952.

Wines, Howie, ed. *Kern County Centennial Almanac.* Bakersfield, CA: Kern County Centennial Observance Committee, 1966.

INDEX

Partners in Progress Index

Bakersfield Californian 138
Bakersfield College 149
Bakersfield Ready Mix, Inc. 142
Bakersfield Sandstone Brick Company 127
Borton, Petrini & Conron 150-151
Brock's Department Store 128-129
Calcot, Ltd. 132
Cassady & Co., Eugene F. 141
Chevron USA, Inc. 147
Denio, Inc., J.L. 124
Floyd's Stores, Inc. 135
Greater Bakersfield Chamber of Commerce 122
Gulf Oil Corporation 148
Icardo Farms 146
KERO-TV23 134
Lufkin's Business College 130
Mercy Hospital 139
Occidental Exploration and Production Company 136
Plank, Realtor, Lloyd E. 143
Rio Bravo Resort 125
San Joaquin Community Hospital 133
Shell California Production Inc. 123
Sullivan's Standard Petroleum Company 140
Tejon Ranch Company 144-145
Tenneco West 131
Tucker Datsun, Wally 126
Wickersham Jewelers 137

Italicized numbers indicate illustrations.

A
Adams, James 27
Alert Hook and Ladder Company 52, *52*
Alexander, David 27, 29
Allen, William 42
Alta California 13, 14, 16, 17, 18
Alverson, Ellen 35
Alverson, Labon 43
Amalgamated Street Railways Employees' Union 77
American Federation of Labor 77
American Legion 84, 94
American Legion Weekly 85
American Revolution 35
American River 21
Anaconda Copper Mine 55
Anheuser-Busch 101
Anza, Juan Bautista de 14
Arizona 21
Arlington Hotel *53*
Arlington House 52, 61, 73
Asphalto (see McKittrick)

B
Bailey, Richard *101*

Baker Turnpike 41
Baker, Constantine 43
Baker, Eliza 35
Baker, Ellen 33
Baker, James 35
Baker, Mary Featherstone 35
Baker, May 33
Baker, Nathan 35
Baker, Nellie 33
Baker, Robert 42
Baker, Thomas 25, 27, 32, 33, 35, 36, *36*, 37, 38, 39, 40, 41, 42, 43, 45, 49, 87, 89
Baker, Tom 33, *37*
Baker, William 35
Bakersfield, becomes county seat 49
Bakersfield, incorporated 45
Bakersfield, naming of 39
Bakersfield & Kern Electric Railway 76
Bakersfield & Sumner Street Railway 59
Bakersfield Building and Loan Association 70
Bakersfield Californian 71, 72, 73, 85, 87, 91, 96
Bakersfield Chamber of Commerce 42, 49, 99
Bakersfield Civic Auditorium 99
Bakersfield Club 42, 49
Bakersfield Echo 65, 87
Bakersfield Electric Company 83
Bakersfield Fire Department 58
Bakersfield Gas and Electric Company 71
Bakersfield Gas Works 59
Bakersfield Junior College 83
Bakersfield Militia *59*
Bakersfield Musical Association 89
Bakersfield Sandstone and Brick Company 62
Bakersfield Telephone Exchange 59
Bakersfield Water Works 59, *70*
Bakersfield (Liberty ship) 84
Bank of Bakersfield 70
Banning, Phineas 27, 29
Barnes, Thomas 29, 41
Beale, Edward 21, 26, 27, *27*, 29, 36, 41, 42
Beale, Mary Edwards 29
Beale, Truxtun 29, *31*, 78
Beale Memorial Clocktower 78, *80*, 95, 99
Belleview Ranch 62
Benecia 35
Bennett, Albert 49
Bishop, Sam 26, 29, 39
Bishop 26
Blacksmith's Union 77
Blake, William 9
Blue Mountain 33
Bodfish 27
Bohna, Caroline 31
Bohna, Christian 30, 31, 32, 33
Bohna, Sarah Louise 31, 33
Bollinger, Marge *101*

Bonaparte, Joseph 16
Bonaparte, Napoleon 16
Bonestell, Louis H. 42
Bonneville, Benjamin 19
Brewers Union 77
Brown, Harvey 36
Brundage, Benjamin 56
Brunk, George 31
Buchanan, James 29, 35
Buena Vista County 27
Buena Vista Lake 10, 11, 29, 35, 36, 41, 55, 58
Buena Vista Ranch 13, *54*
Burrell, Alfred 49
Butterfield, John 29
Butterfield Overland Line 29, 37
Buttonwillow 80
Buttonwillow Bird Lady (see Fanny Tracy)

C
Cajon Pass 17
Calaveras River 16
Caliente 50
California Cotton Growers and Manufacturers Association 42, 43
California Oil World 79
California State College, Bakersfield 100, 101
California Trail 23
Calloway, Oliver 55
Calloway Canal 56
Camp, William 87
Camp Babbitt 37
Canfield, Wellington 42
Carpenter, William *101*
Carr, Billy 53, 55, 56, 57, 58, 62, 63, 68
Carson, Frank 65
Carson, Kit 19, *19*, 21
Catholics 43
Central Pacific Railroad 39, 47, 49
Central Park 30, 39
Charles III 13
Chester, George 39, 43, 49
Chester, Julius 39, 40, 42, 56
Chiles, Joseph 19
Chinese Joss House 67
Chinese Ying Ming Hall 98
Christian Towers 101
Cigar Makers Union 77
Civil Air Patrol 93
Civil War 27, 29, 30, 36, 37, 38
Clear Creek Canyon 38
Colorado 21
Colorado River 14, 16, 18, 20, 29
Columbia River 18, 20
Comanches 19
Continental Divide 16
Cortez, Hernando 13
Cotton Experiment Station 87
Cozby, Pat 97

Crawford Bar 79
Crosstown Freeway 99
Cuen, Ventura 24
Cumming's Valley 15
Curran, James 62

D

Daily Alta California 26
Daugherty, Bill 31
Davis, Jefferson 29
Day, Jim 96
Deering, Alexander 49
Delano, Columbus 49
Delano 14, *48*, 49, 80
Depression, The 91, 92
Depression of 1873 49
Derby, George H. 23
Desert Land Act 56, 58
Doheny, Edward 76
Donner Party 31
Dorris, Grace 87
Dorsey, Jesse 85
Douglan, Sholto 65

E

Earthquake of 1952 94, *94*, 95, *95*, 96, 97, *97*
Echeandia, Jose 17
El Camino Real 14
El Camino Viejo 23
El Gobernador 43
Elizabeth Lake 23
Elwood, James 75
Elwood, Jonathan 75

F

Fages, Pedro 13, 23
Ferdinand VII 16
Fergusson, S.W. 63, 68
Fillmore, Millard 26
Fire of 1883 58
Fire of 1889 61
First Baptist Church 67
First Congregational Church 67
Fitzgerald, Thomas 28, 30
Flood of 1893 67
Font, Pedro 14
Foothill High School 99
Fort Defiance 29
Fort Tejon 26, 27, *28*, 29, 36, 37
Fort Vancouver 18
Frémont, John C. *12*, 20, 21, 28
French Hotel 49, 53, 59
Fresno 47

G

Galvez, Jose de 13
Galyen, LeRoy 85
Garcés, Francisco 14, *14*, 15, 16, 19
Germans, imprisonment of 93
Gifford, Frank *103*

Gilbert, Robert 31
Gilroy 19
Glennville 27, 28
Godey, Alexis 21
Gold Rush, California 24, 35
Gold Rush, Kern 27, 42
Golden State Highway 89
Gordon, Aneas 25
Gordon's Ferry 10, 25, 57, 75
Goshen 49
Granados, Eva *101*
Grand Hotel *86*
Grant, Ulysses S. 56
Grayson, Horace 97
Great Basin 21
Great Railroad Strike of 1894 68
Great Salt Lake 18, 19
Great Southern Overland Mail (see Butterfield Overland Line)
Greenhorn Mountains 19, 21, 27, 28, 33, 38, 42

H

Haggin, James 53, 55, 56, 57, 58, 59, 62, 63, 68
Halaumne 11
Hall, Leonard 92
Hammel, Henry 39
Harpending, Asbury 38
Harrell, Alfred 67, 71, 72, 87, 91
Harris, Jim 31
Hart, Don 100
Hart Park 10
Havilah 27, 38, 39, 49
Havilah Courier 42
Hawsu 10
Hayes, Rutherford 56
Hearst, George 55
Helm, George *79*
Henry, James 38
Historical Preservation Commission 103
Hogeye 27
Homestake Gold Mine 55
Hood, William 50
Hoover, Herbert 85
Hot Springs Valley 38
Hudnut, Richard 42, 43, 49, 56
Hudson's Bay Company 18

I

Independent Oil Producers Agency 78, 79
Indian Commission 24
Irving, Washington 19
Isabella Dam 98

J

Jackson, Andrew R. 40, 42, 43
Jackson Ranch *55*
Jacoby, Morris 43
Jameson, Charlotte 36

Japanese, imprisonment of 93
Jastro, Henry 43, 51, 68, 70, 71
Jastro's Brewery 53
Jewett, Philo 37, 38, 39, 42
Jewett, Solomon 29, 37, 38, 42, 49, 70
Johnson, John 38
Johnston, James 42
Jones, Augustus 42
Jones, William 37

K

Kansas Pacific Railroad 39
Karlen, Russell 99, 100
Kaweah River 25
Kelawatsets 18
Kern, Edward 21
Kern 76
Kern County, formation of 39
Kern County Agricultural Society 42, 46
Kern County Airport (see Meadows Field)
Kern County Board of Trade 89
Kern County Californian 56
Kern County Centennial 100
Kern County Chamber of Commerce 89
Kern County Council of Labor 77
Kern County Courier 42, 43, 49, 51
Kern County Courthouse *50*, 51, *71*, 81
Kern County Defense Council 92
Kern County Echo 56
Kern County Equipment Company 97
Kern County Gazette 50, 61
Kern County Grand Jury 85
Kern County High School 67, *69*, 89
Kern County Historical Society 91
Kern County Jail 83
Kern County Land Company 63, 64, *64*, 65, 68, 70, *70*, 71, 73, 80
Kern County Museum 31, 84, 99
Kern Delta 29, 30, 32, 42, 43, 45, 46, 53, 55, 63
Kern Fair Association 83
Kern Island 28, 30, 32, 33, 36, 37, 39, 55, 56
Kern Island Canal 39, 47, *48*, *66*
Kern Island Dairy 57
Kern Island Irrigation Company 42
Kern Lake 9, 10, 11, 24, 25, 29, 30, 35, 37
Kern River 10, 11, *11*, 14, 15, 16, 18, 19, 20, 21, 25, *26*, 27, 28, 36, 41, 49, 53, 55, 56, 57, 58, 67, 75, 79
Kern River Flour Mill 43
Kern River Land & Canal Company 56
Kern River Oil Field 76, 78
Kern Valley Bank 52, 59, 70
Kern Valley Water Company 53
Kernville 42
Keyes, Richard 27
Keyes Mine 27
Keyesville 27
Kings River 35

Knight's Ferry 18
K'ono-likin 10
Ku Klux Klan 85

L
Lake Tahoe 20
Lakeview No. 1 83, *83*
Landers, William 42
Lang 51
Lathrop 47
Lebec 27
Lebec Tree *28*
Ledbetter, Edna 97
Lincoln, Abraham 36, 38
Livermore, Horatio 40, 42, 43, 46, 47, 53, 55
Lockheed Aircraft Component Factories 93
Los Angeles 23, 27, 29, 30, 37, 51, 76, 84
Los Angeles-Stockton Road 25, 26
Love, Harry 25
Low, Frederick 40
Lux, Charles 55, 56, 57, 58, 59
Lux vs. Haggin 57

M
Mason, John (see John Monroe)
Masons 43, 45, 49, 76
McCauley, Spotty (see James Henry)
McCray, Alexander 28, 29
McCray, John 28
McKeadney, Hugh 43
McKenzie, James 31
McKinney, James 78, 89
McKittrick 75
McWorter, Milton 75
Meadows, Cecil 89, 93
Meadows Field 89, *89*, 98
Means, Tom 75, 76, *76*
Mears, Rick *102*
Memorial Hospital 31
Merced 47
Merced River 16
Methodists 43
Metropolitan Opera 89
Mexican War 31
Mexico 13, 14, 16, 17, 19, 20, 21
Meyer, Daniel 62
Midway Sunset Oil Fields *74*, 81
Miller, Fred, *101*
Miller, Henry 55, 56, *56*, 57, 58, 59
Millerton 27
Mills, Alex 51
Minter Field 93
Mission San Gabriel 17
Mission San Juan Baptista 16
Mississippi River 10
Modesto 47
Mojave Desert 11, 16, 18, 51
Mokelumne River 16
Mono Lake 19

Monroe, John 38
Monterey 13, 14, 16, 18
Montgomery, Joseph 35, 36
Montgomery, William 35, 36
Mooney, Maggie 65
Moraga, Gabriel 16
Motel Bakersfield *93*
Mount Whitney 10
Mount Zion Baptist Church 67
Mountain View Dairy *57*
Murieta, Joaquin 25, 26

N
National Grange 45
Nevada 18, 21
New Deal 91
New Mexico 21
Niederaur, Philip *58*
Nordoff, Charles 45

O
Oak Creek Pass 15
Odd Fellows, International Order of 43, 45, 49
Ohio Oil Company 98
Oil Strike of 1921 86
Oildale 89
Old Spanish Trail 20, 23
Old Stage Hotel 53
Ontario Silver Mine 55
Oregon 20, 33
Oregon Trail 20
Owens, Buck *103*

P
Pacheco, Mabel 65
Pacheco, Romualdo 65
Packard, Jeff 78
Palmer, William 39
Paloma Refinery 95
Paloma Well 98
Panic of 1857 36
Patterson, John 29
People's Railroad (see San Francisco & San Joaquin Valley Railroad)
Pifer, Phil 97
Pioneer Canal *47*
Polk, James 21
Portolá, Gaspar de 13
Poso Ranch *54*
Power Development Company 70, 71
Power, Transit, and Light Company 76
Producer's Savings Bank 70
Prohibition 91
Public Works Administration 91

Q
Quartzburg 27

R
Railroad Avenue School 53, 67

Rancho Castaic 24
Rancho El Tejon 24
Rancho La Liebre 24, 29
Rancho Los Alamos 24
Rancho San Emigdio 24, *24*, 58
Randsburg *73*
Redington, John 42, 43, 46, 47, 53, 55
Reeder, Lewis 33
Republic of California 21
Rhymes, James 39
Ridge Route Road 84, 86
Rio Bravo Cotton Gin *87*
Rio Bravo Tennis Ranch 101
Rio de San Felipe (see Kern River)
Rocky Mountains 16, 18, 19, 20
Roosevelt, Franklin 91
Rose, Allen 31
Rosedale 80
Route 99 30, *85*, 99, 100

S
San Andreas Fault 9
San Antonio 29
San Bernardino Valley 17, 18
San Diego 13
San Emigdio 23, 29
San Francisco 10, 24, 29, 30, 47, 49, 63, 72
San Francisco & San Joaquin Valley Railroad 72, 75
San Francisco Chronicle 56
San Francisquito Canyon 23
San Gabriel 14
San Joaquin Community Hospital 83, 101
San Joaquin Light and Power Company 83
San Joaquin River 16, 35, 47
San Jose 21
Sanger, Gustave 42
Santa Fe 19
Santa Fe Railroad 77
Sargent, Aaron 56
Saturday Evening Post 96
Schurz, Carl 56
Scribner, George 59
Scribner Water Works 71
Scribner's Opera House 59
Sebastian Indian Reservation 26, 27, 32
Serra, Junípero 13
Shafter, William 68
Shell, Mary 101
Shirley, Walker 31
Sholo 10
Sierra Nevadas 9, 18, 19, 20, 21, 23, 31, 95, 96
Skiles, James 31, 37
Skiles, Thomas 38
Smith, Jedediah 16, 17, 18, *18*, 19
Smith, Sylvester 56, 81
Soledad Canyon 51
Sonora 14, 24

Souther, William 46, 47
Southern Californian 56
Southern Hotel 59, 61, 62, *62, 65, 96*
Southern Pacific 43, *43,* 46, 47, 49, 50, 51, 55, 63, 64, 68, 71, 72, 77
Spanish American War 68, 72
St. Clair, Leonard 71
St. John's Episcopal Mission 64
St. Louis 19, 29
St. Paul's Episcopal Church 61
Stanford, Leland 49
Stanislaus River 16, 18
State Highway Commission 84
Stevens, Elisha 31, 33
Stockdale 80
Stockdale Country Club 65
Stockdale Industrial Park 101
Stockdale Village Shopping Center 101
Stockton 23, 35, 47
Sullivan, Frank 98, 99
Sumner, Charles 50
Sumner 40, 43, 68
Sunset Oil Field 77, *82*
Sunset Railroad 77, 81
Sutter's Fort 20
Sutter's Mill 21
Swamp and Overflow Lands Act of 1857 35
Sylvester, Robert 93
Sylvester, William 93

T
Taft, William 81
Tehachapi 43, 49, 51, *51,* 65, 95
Tehachapi Loop 50
Tehachapi Mountain 24
Tehachapi Pass 20, 50, 51
Tehachapi Valley 15
Tejon Canyon 23, 26
Telegraph Stage Company 43
Television: KBAK 98; KERO 98; KGET 98

Tenneco West 100, 101
Tevis, Lloyd 53, 56, 57, 58, 59, 63, 65, 68
Tevis, William 65
Texas 20, 21
Three Fingered Jack 25
Three Rivers 24
Tibbet, Burt 78
Tibbet, Lawrence 89
Tibbet, Will 78, 89
Town Ditch 36
Town Hall 43, 45, 49, 52
Tracy, Fanny *87*
Tracy, Ferdinand 42
Treaty of Ghent 16
Treaty of Guadalupe Hidalgo 21, 24
Troy, Daniel 42
Truckee River 21
T'sinleu 10, 26
Tuhoumne 11
Tulare 47, 49
Tulare County 24
Tulare Lake 10, 35, 55
Tulare Times 41
Tuolumne River 16
Typhoid Epidemic 43

U
U.S. Camel Corps 29
U.S. Coast and Geodetic Survey 96
U.S. Land Office 35
U.S. Topographical Corps 9, 20, 23, 26, 39
Union Cemetery 43
Union Pacific 63
Utah 21

V
Vega Aircraft Company 93
Visalia 25, 35, 37, 47, 49
Visalia Land Office 56

W
Wakayama (Bakersfield's Sister City) 99, 100
Walker, Joseph Reddeford 19, 21, 28
Walker Lake 21
Walker's Pass 19
Wallace, Richard 101
War of 1812 16
Warren, Earl 97, *97, 103*
Wasco 80
Wawcoye 10
Wear, George 61
Weeks, George 71, 72
Weill, Alphonse 59
Wells Fargo and Company 55
White River 14, 24, 27
White Wolf Fault 96
Wible, Simon 70
Wicker, Corbin 31
Williamson, Robert 26
Winer, Gene 99
Woilu 10, 18, 30, 32, 33
Women's suffrage 87
Woods, John 25
Woodsville 25
Woody, Sparrel 31, 33
Woody 14, 33
Works Progress Administration 91
World War I 84
World War II 92, 93, 94
Wyoming 21

Y
Yoakum, William 42
Yokuts 10, 11, 14, 18, 26, 30
Young, Ewing 19
Young, George 42
Yowlumne 10, 18, 21
Yuma 14, 15

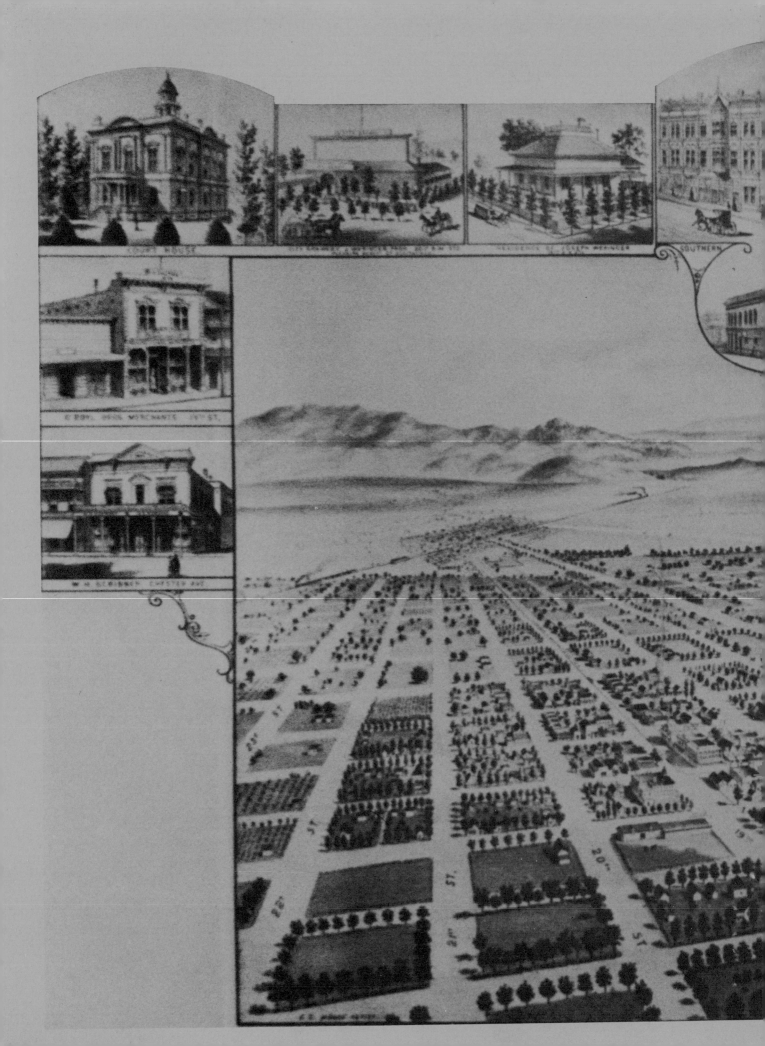